Kirkus Indie Review (Oct 2016): "McClung has written a thoughtful think piece that also serves as a touching tribute to 'one of my greatest teachers during the worst time of her life.' ... The questions the author presents readers arise appropriately from her narrative and also have universal relevance, including 'When is the last time you said you were sorry to yourself or to another?' ... McClung offers many well-sketched, even funny, anecdotes, including her 'outburst' in Target by phone with Rob about buying her outfit ... Heartfelt reflections on the lessons and strength to be gained from grief and loss."

Also by Joffre McClung

How Learning to Say Goodbye Taught Me How to Live
(A Spiritual Memoir)
Balboa Press 2015

The Heart
of the Matter

A **Workbook** and **Guide** to
Finding Your Way Back to **Self-Love**

JOFFRE MCCLUNG

BALBOA.
PRESS
A DIVISION OF HAY HOUSE

Balboa Press books may be ordered through booksellers or by contacting:

Balboa Press
A Division of Hay House
1663 Liberty Drive
Bloomington, IN 47403
www.balboapress.com
1 (877) 407-4847

Because of the dynamic nature of the Internet, any web addresses or
links contained in this book may have changed since publication and
may no longer be valid. The views expressed in this work are solely those
of the author and do not necessarily reflect the views of the publisher,
and the publisher hereby disclaims any responsibility for them.

The author of this book does not dispense medical advice or prescribe
the use of any technique as a form of treatment for physical, emotional,
or medical problems without the advice of a physician, either directly
or indirectly. The intent of the author is only to offer information
of a general nature to help you in your quest for emotional and
spiritual well-being. In the event you use any of the information in
this book for yourself, which is your constitutional right, the author
and the publisher assume no responsibility for your actions.

Any people depicted in stock imagery provided by Thinkstock are
models, and such images are being used for illustrative purposes only.
Certain stock imagery © Thinkstock.

Print information available on the last page.

ISBN: 978-1-5043-7509-2 (sc)
ISBN: 978-1-5043-7511-5 (hc)
ISBN: 978-1-5043-7510-8 (e)

Balboa Press rev. date: 03/03/2017

To all the people
who long for a more loving
and compassionate world
and are not sure where to start.

That's me

Contents

Part 3:
Investigating, Interrogating, and Integrating

Acknowledgments

I am grateful to all the teachers and authors that have opened my heart and expanded my mind throughout the years. Your wisdom and courage to share your journey and perspective made this book possible.

I would also like to thank my friends and guides, both seen and unseen, that have walked beside me though the good times and bad times, always encouraging me to continue moving toward love even when it felt impossible. Your unwavering love, support, and guidance transformed my life.

Lastly, I am most grateful to my Higher Self. Through her love and wisdom, she empowered me to find the love I had for myself that had been buried long ago, and inspired me to honor and celebrate that love in all that I do.

Preface

My intention for writing this book grew out of my first book: *How Learning to Say Goodbye Taught Me How to Live (A Spiritual Memoir)*. In that book, I chronicled the inner work my best friend and I did during her battle with cancer to stay conscious and grow despite our pain.

When I wrote that book, I had just come out of an eight-year period of loss that had stripped me bare of everything that had come to define me outwardly as well as inwardly. I used that period of pain and emotional rawness to finish healing and integrating my remaining inner wounded parts—or orphans, as I call them. I worked daily, removing all the lies and negative beliefs my life had been built on thus far by replacing them with more loving and expanding beliefs.

While my intention for that book was to remind people of the spiritual lessons and gifts one may encounter during a crisis and offer reminders to stay focused on growth during dark times, the book did something very different for me. Because I was writing the book while my friend was dying, I didn't see the message till after she had passed.

When I went back and read it later, I saw with great clarity that underneath all the lessons and the gifts we moved through during that time was the recurring theme of self-love. You are either moving through the world in self-love or you are not. Once I had some distance from that painful period, I saw clearly that what I had actually done through my inner exploration, healing, and integration process was reclaim my self-love.

With this new perspective, I had to acknowledge that while the memoir could be very helpful to those on the path of personal and spiritual growth—especially for those helping someone with a terminal diagnosis—it did not address how one gets to a place of self-awareness and self-love. It had been written for those already well on their way.

In all fairness, I was not in a place to share how I had returned to self-love at that time. I was still recovering from all the previous losses, with one more death still looming over me. My sole purpose for that book was to help people stay awake and choose love over fear during a crisis, with a side benefit of giving me a wider perspective during that sad time. Little did I know then that the universe had another agenda.

With some time between me and all the death and losses I had experienced, I began to wonder, "What about those who are just starting out or those who are hitting a wall in their growth? How can anyone expect people to stay self-aware and rooted in love during a crisis when they are moving through their daily lives unaware that they have little or no self-love? Without self-awareness and self-love, I could not have handled my friend's critical situation and stayed focused on choosing love over fear.

That is when I understood that my first book was actually a sequel to a book I had not even written yet! The universe indeed had an agenda, even though it seemed a bit backwards to me.

Of course I now know I could not have written this book until I had written *How Learning to say Goodbye Taught Me How to Live.* I am by nature a fairly private person—especially when it comes to something so intimate as a personal spiritual journey. I am one of those people who prefer to walk it rather than talk it. I could not have shared what is in this book without having gone through the process of writing that first book. I guess you could say the universe knew in its infinite wisdom that backward was the way to go with me. I needed to get my feet wet before I would be willing to jump in all the way.

Although I had kept my inner work fairly private, I had shared my journey and process back to self-love with a few close friends. When I saw them use this information in their homework with great results, I knew it was time to jump in all the way. I figured that if it helped one person move forward in reclaiming self-love, then it would be worth sharing my inner process.

The processes and techniques in this book came out of my thirty years on the path of spiritual personal growth. They are simply what finally worked to free me from my past and allow me to reclaim my self-love. My hope is that the information in this book will do the same for you and you won't have to spend years working to get there, as I did.

Introduction

I cannot teach anybody anything.
I can only make them think.
—Socrates

Self-love or the lack of self-love not only determines how we see ourselves but also governs how we experience the world around us. It is the prism through which we see and define all things. So why do so few of us see self-love as the starting point to our inner and outer health? Oh, we tell children to like themselves, but how do we teach them to do that when we don't practice it ourselves? When you ask people if they love themselves and how they do that, they often will say, "Yes, I love myself," and then they will likely provide an example of an action, such as, "I take a spa day," "I buy myself something I have wanted," or "I eat only healthy foods." I have rarely heard someone respond with "Yes, I am compassionate with myself," "I value myself at all times," or "I am kind and forgiving with myself." While taking a spa day or eating what gives you pleasure can be helpful and loving, these things are in no way indicative of someone who is necessarily rooted in self-love.

While self-love can propel us to take loving actions, self-love is not an action but a state of being. When you reside in that loving state, it is with you at all times wherever you go, and it can never be diminished or taken away by outside influences. Just as negativity or darkness can permeate every nook and cranny of your existence if you allow them to, self-love can and will permeate your entire existence if you will heal and transform what has separated you from the truth of self-love.

My mission with this book is to get you to look at self-love with new eyes in order to understand that it is your right to reclaim your self-love. Also, I want to help you connect the dots to what has separated you from your own love so you can be empowered to rediscover it.

This book is not a big book for a reason. I wanted it to be less about me and more about you. After all, it is your personal journey toward the truth, not mine. That is why it is written in a workbook format. I know some may want a step-by-step, two-week process that they can complete and be done with it so they can move on, but that is not how it works.

Personal growth takes time, diligence, and patience. It cannot be achieved by doing one meditation or a couple of exercises. You have had years to reinforce your lack of self-love and the negative beliefs that grew out of it. So, understandably, it is going to take some time and focus for you to untangle yourself from the lies you have believed for so long and move back into self-love.

My experience with inner healing has shown me that it must be done in layers so you can absorb the understanding before you move onto the next layer needing healing and transformation. This is not to make it drawn out for the universe's amusement but rather to allow you to grow in your wisdom, thus empowering you along the path toward wholeness.

It is your job on the path back to self-love to become intimate with yourself and to learn what makes you tick. I know that can sound silly, and I can hear some shouting, "Are you crazy? Of course I know myself!" But I would counter, "Do you know why you react as you do to certain emotional triggers? Do you know why you feel powerless? Do you know why you make decisions that never seem to be in your best interest? Do you know why you put off your own happiness for another's happiness? Do you know why you keep experiencing the same negative energy over and over again, just in new clothes?"

As spiritual beings, it is our job to investigate, interrogate and eventually integrate everything going on inside of us. While that can seem daunting, just know you have everything you need inside of you to do this sacred work. Much like a detective on a case, you will become adept at investigating what is happening inside of you. You will be amazed at how much information will be revealed simply by consciously observing and taking notes on what is going on inside of you throughout your day. You will teach yourself how to interrogate the various parts of yourself and push past the first response to the truth that lies underneath. You will discover the power that is inherent in the simple word *why*.

Through the process of investigating and interrogating, you will begin to integrate those parts of yourself that have been orphaned and lost, bringing them back to the whole through understanding and love. While it can seem difficult, just know that it is the most fulfilling work you can do.

Some of you may now be wondering what my job in this relationship will be if you are going to do all the work. After all, I wrote the book; I must have some responsibilities. And I do. As the Socrates quote said, my job is to make you think. And that includes not only helping you to discover what you truly *think* about yourself and the world around you but also helping you redefine what self-love means.

I would also add one caveat to the Socrates quote. My job is not only to make you *think* but, even more importantly, to make you *feel*. Self-love, as is all love, is anchored in your heart. So besides guiding you to investigate through the use of questions—the big whys—I will do my best to aid you in understanding the importance of your emotions and how to become comfortable with your emotions and even befriend them for your detective work. It is only through becoming emotionally adept that you can make lasting changes within and return to your natural state of self-love.

I have divided the book into three parts. The first part introduces you to the tools you will be using on your journey back to self-love.

Think of it as being like the warm-up you do before you hit the gym floor or go for a long run. Just as skipping a warm-up can make your workout more difficult, not working with the tools will make your work in the second and third parts more difficult and lead to less favorable results. The work you will be doing in the first part is actually laying down the foundation for which all the work to follow will be built upon. So even if you are familiar with the various tools, go ahead and reacquaint yourself with them again. You never know what you might learn.

The second part is where we begin the workout. It focuses on describing and working with the three components of self-love. It begins the process of self-discovery and becoming aware of what you believe, as well as what you feel inside. It is also where you will begin to redefine love for yourself.

The third part leads you deeper within the exploration to the healing and integration processes. It is where you will use your emotions to explore your inner landscape and meet those orphaned parts of yourself. It is also where you will begin to integrate those parts back into the whole through compassionate understanding, forgiveness, and love.

All the chapters in the three parts include questions that you will ask yourself to get a better understanding of why you think and feel the way you do. I have left space for you to journal your thoughts and feelings to each question, but feel free to work with them as you deem fit.

No matter how you work through the questions, be as detailed as you possibly can in your answers. The more you know about what you are thinking and feeling, the better. Some of the questions appear to require only one-word responses, but I want you to go deeper. After you write down your answer of yes or no, I want you describe why you answered the way you did. For example, if you answer yes to "Is working toward reclaiming your self-love selfish?" you should include all the reasons you believe that to be true. It is not good enough to say, "Because it *is* true." Look within to find out why you believe it to be true. For example, "It is wrong to put myself before others" or "because self-love can cause me to become narcissistic."

Begin to always push past the first response and reveal to yourself why you believe what you believe or why you feel the way you do. The questions are to aid you in self-discovery, so do yourself a favor and be as truthful and as detailed as you can.

Treat it as an investigation and investigate! Push for the truth. There are no right or wrong answers; there is only the truth. The questions will greatly aid you in beginning to understand how you got where you are and help reveal the lies you have been telling yourself.

Following the questions are meditation exercises. If meditation is new or foreign to you, don't worry. I will go over what I mean by meditation in the first part on the tools. By the time you finish the first exercise, some of the mystery should dissipate. Meditation is simply a technique you will use to engage the essential tool of imagination.

While the questions are meant to get you thinking, the exercises are meant to get you *feeling*. You cannot just think your way into self-love. You must also *feel* your way there. Although it is important to use your mind to garner understanding, it is only through transforming the wounds and barriers around your heart that you will find your way back to self-love.

Please know you have the freedom to do the meditations in a way that works for you. The details or images in the meditations are meant as suggestions, just as are the affirmations in the "Your Homework" section. So don't feel obligated to follow them to the letter. They are designed to stimulate and open up your imagination as well as to offer examples of how you might navigate certain issues and terrain.

Look at them as jumping-off points. Nothing would thrill me more than someone telling me that he or she read the meditation and, when he or she went within, the meditation took on a life of its own. That's exactly as it should be. Wise people know they are not only the students but the teachers too. So allow the meditations and affirmations to become your own. All of the work in this book is to empower you, so you decide what works and is right for you.

I have no rules on how you do your inner work, with two exceptions. First, you must be truthful with yourself. That alone will take some practice. Most of us have gotten excellent at believing our lies about ourselves and the world around us. You will get better at knowing when you are lying to yourself as you work with your emotions. This brings us to the second exception: you must be willing to *feel*. Emotions are one of your best navigational tools. So use them! Also know you cannot change a belief if you are not prepared to release the feelings that implanted that belief in your heart to begin with; nor can you implant a new belief without also feeling it in your heart.

Following the meditation is the "Your Homework" section for the week. Let me be clear here: simply because I said it is for a week does not mean you will do it for a week and then be free to toss it aside. You are going to be returning to certain work or exercises over and over during your process of reclaiming your self-love. The suggestion of doing it for a week is to keep you focused on what you have begun to uncover in that particular chapter and to set a pattern of being diligent with your inner work. It is also a way to have you practice being self-aware throughout your daily life. I want you to become a spiritual detective of your life—and that means all facets of your life, not just the hour or so you set aside for your personal growth.

I have included a page for notes at the very end of each chapter. You can use the page for whatever you like. We are all different, and the way we work will be different. Some may like to keep notes on what new information they discover while moving through their day. Others may prefer to journal about their inner meditative excursions. Some may want to use it to summarize what the work in that chapter revealed. It can also be used to go into more detail with a particular answer in the questions section. It doesn't matter how you use it or even if you chose not to use it. I have included it so those that like to write, list, or journal can do so and have it conveniently within the book so they can return to it at any time.

I also want to mention that I use the words *the universe, the divine*, and *God* interchangeably. Don't let my use of a certain word stop you from getting the overall message. If you don't like it when "the universe" is used instead of "god," or vice versa, just change it. However, do take note of your discomfort and investigate the reasons behind it.

Your ego will be activated through some, if not all, of the work. That is a good thing! You will begin to see how your ego works and how quickly you believe the first answer you receive to a question, how quickly you stop at the first image you see during meditation, or how quickly you stop doing the homework. Almost always, at least in the beginning of your detective work, the first answer or image is not the bottom line. However, that is okay if you use it as a way to differentiate between your ego voice and the truth within.

By becoming a spiritual detective, you will begin to not only challenge what your life was built on, but more importantly, you will discover that you have the power *to choose* what you will build your life on from this moment forward.

Returning to self-love is the ultimate self-empowering act. Once you realize that you can heal and transform yourself and that you *can* choose how you want to see the world and the universe, you are finally claiming your authentic power. And when you use that power to choose self-love, you will stop being an unconscious victim to your past and will become the conscious creator of your future that you were always meant to be.

Part 1

The Three Essential Tools

Chapter 1

What is meditation, and why is it important to engage the imagination?

Meditation is simply focusing your attention. However, when you combine attention with imagination, you can become the healer and architect of your life.

In the past twenty years, meditation has gone mainstream. What at one time was considered a practice only for certain religions or New Agers is now being discussed as a healthy practice by doctors, teachers, and others as a way to decompress and become centered.

So what do I mean when I use the word *meditation*? Meditation is just the focusing of your attention. Period. Meditation is a way for you to slow down your ego chatter (head chatter), move out of your logical mind, and move into your inner world, where the real work is done. All that is required is an intention to be present and practice. You can meditate lying down, sitting up, in the tub (great for emotional clearings), on the bed, or even while walking. Once you become proficient, you can even do it on a subway!

However, in the beginning, I would suggest it be done in silence or with music. I often used instrumental music that matched the emotion I was working to bring forth. Music can be one of the most helpful tools to get you out of your logical mind and move you into your emotions. Music can lift you out of the everyday and transport you to your inner world. There is no quicker way to connect to your imagination than through the language of music, and you are going to need your imagination for much of your inner work. So I recommend using it—especially if you are a very logic-centered person.

There are many types of meditations. Centering or quieting meditations are the types most people identify with when discussing mediation. They entail focusing on your breath and quieting your mind for a period. The idea is to free yourself from all thoughts and feelings in the moment and put your focus on taking deep, slow breaths. Some people will focus on an image in their mind's eye. Others focus on relaxing each muscle, starting at their feet and slowly rising to the top of their head. Still others like to repeat a mantra, allowing them to go deeper into their quiet center. Centering meditations are a great way to calm down, quiet the ego voice, and become grounded. However, they are not the only types of meditations.

By using creative visualization techniques—or, simply put, your imagination—meditations become a way into your inner landscape, where all healing begins. Creative visualization meditation is simply using your imagination to visualize what is happening inside of you. We all have used creative visualization in some form or other in the past. If you have ever spent some time daydreaming (a powerful creating meditation), you have used creative visualization.

I call creative visualization meditations working meditations because during such meditations you are meditating with the intention of connecting to the various parts of yourself. Working meditations can be used to heal childhood wounds, confront your shadow aspects, connect with your Higher Self, converse with the universe, release fears, uncover beliefs, feel love, do vital emotional clearings, and so much more. The sky is the limit when we engage our birthright to imagine.

I start my working meditations the same way I begin my centering meditations—with breath and moving out of my logical mind. But instead of ignoring the feelings or voices, I follow them to their sources. I use my imagination to see where a voice is originating from or what a feeling looks like and who within me is feeling that way, and then I stay there and work.

By "work" I mean I envision the voices and feelings as separate beings or energies or symbols, and I listen to them and dialogue with them in my mind. For example, if I were emotionally triggered outwardly by something that touches an old unhealed childhood wound, I would envision the inner orphan in meditation and listen to his or her pain or fear and slowly begin to show him or her love, compassion, and empathy. Whatever the orphan feels is missing, I offer it to him or her. If the orphan is afraid, I offer him or her my hand and walk through that fear with him or her. Don't worry; this will make more sense as we get further into the work.

I do want to mention that being in meditation does not mean you will not be aware of what is around you. I have heard people use the excuse "I don't have a quiet place to meditate." Yes, it is helpful to have a quiet, secluded place to begin your practice, but it really doesn't matter. I have been in meditation, clearing pain or anger or fear, when my neighbors above me started stomping above my head. Instead of stopping my meditation, I used my frustration at what was going on above me to move deeper into the emotion I was working with. My belief is that life is in my favor, so if I was getting pissed off from the sounds around me, I knew to push deeper into my frustration and anger and discover what was hiding underneath those emotions. Those "disruptions" actually became instigators for me to go deeper into my emotions and learn more about myself. So as much as the disruptions may have pissed me off, they were always gifts that arrived at the perfect moment.

The other excuse I hear often is "I can't keep my mind focused." Well, guess what, no one can when first starting out. That is why we call it a practice. You have to practice! You may only be able to focus for a minute or two in the beginning, but your focus will grow with time. Just be compassionate with yourself. Remember: You're not being graded or judged. You are not a failure if you allow your mind to wander. Just take note of where it tends to wander off to and when it wanders. These will be huge clues as to what your ego thinks is important, as well as how your ego works to distract you. The point of the work is to learn about all the parts of yourself, and that includes how your ego works.

For example, I would be in the tub doing some healing work on my orphan when I would suddenly realize I had just spent ten minutes giving a self-righteous speech in my head about why the world is screwed up, or twenty minutes rearranging and decorating a room. Sounds crazy and not of much use, right? Wrong! Those diversions taught me a lot about myself and my ego. If I was experiencing self-righteousness, I realized I was actually feeling powerless. One of my ego's reactions to feeling powerless is self-righteousness. If I was decorating a room, I knew that my ego did not want me to deal with the issue I was working on or feel the pain I had just uncovered. Ego wants to keep the status quo at all costs, and mine was a pro at it.

One of your primary jobs in your inner work is to be the detective: to take notes and to follow leads. So don't waste time berating yourself for losing focus. Do take note of the berating, however, because that is an excellent clue as to how you treat and judge yourself, and you will be able to use that information later when you are working on self-love.

If you do lose focus, just take a breath, refocus, and begin again. Your inner world is not going anywhere. It will always be waiting for you to return. You just have to find the courage to begin again.

QUESTIONS TO INVESTIGATE

1) What are your thoughts about meditation?

It is very helpful

2) What are your *feelings* about meditation?

I know that I can use it

3) Have you ever tried meditating? If so, how did it go? If not, why not?

Smetines its good Sometimes its great Sometimes I cant

4) Can you believe meditation can be a tool for self-discovery and healing? If yes, why? If no, why not?

Yes

_____

_____

_____

5) How comfortable are you with engaging with your imagination?

Very

_____

_____

_____

6) Have you ever looked at your imagination as a gift? If not, why not?

Yes because it has always been a place of escape for me.

_____

_____

7) Is your imagination an important part of you, or do you see it as frivolous? Why do you see it the way you do?

It is a way for me to escape provide hope for myself. A reminder of the power of God and that there is more!

8) Can you remember a time when you used your imagination in a negative way, such as envisioning a worst-case scenario? Describe how you used it then.

Yes, I often imagine releasing my anger and yelling at the people that I work with + the kids that I work with and people in general

9) Can you remember a time when you used your imagination in a positive way, such as daydreaming a new dream for yourself? Describe how you used it then.

Yes, I often dream of marrying and dancing with the man that God has for me as a reminder that God has a soul-mate for me.

10) Have you ever considered that there is an inner world inside of you with all the answers to all your questions? If not, why not?

No, I like to think that God has all of the answers and he speaks to me.

11) How open are you to exploring this inner world?

All ways

12) Does the idea of entering your inner world frighten you? If so, why?

It used to until I learned how to do shadow work. + it's benefits

13) How might your world change if you discovered this inner world?

I think if I tapped into it more often I would be more grounded.

Meditation Exercise

(As with all the meditations included in this book, please read the exercise in its entirety before you begin.)

A good visualization exercise is to create an inner safe and loving place. You didn't think I was going to just talk about meditation, did you? You will use this safe space each time we do a meditation exercise at the end of each chapter, so it is important that you create it before we go any further. If you already have a meditation practice, use this exercise to expand your safe space, adding more elements that invoke feelings of love. I have never met anyone who can't benefit by expanding his or her capacity to feel love.

Once you have taken a few deep, slow breaths and are centered and focused on the present (not worrying about your grocery list or job), allow your imagination to begin to create your inner safe place. Just play at it like a child would, not worrying if you are doing it right or wrong.

Just enjoy the process of creating an inner landscape using your imagination with no limits. It doesn't matter how the landscape looks. Some people may see mountains; others, trees or beaches. Still others may see a church or an ancient temple. Make it up! It can't be wrong, since anything you make up is coming from your subconscious anyway. Moreover, what your subconscious reveals is a tremendous boon to your detective work of getting to know yourself.

Stay with the initial image, adding as many elements as you wish. See the sky (if there is a sky). Is it full of stars or perhaps a moon? Is there water nearby? Are there rocks or cliffs? Are there animals milling about? If you are in a building, what is it made out of? Is it smooth and shiny or rough? Is it new or ancient? Is it open to the sky, or does it have windows? Go wild. It is your safe space, so add all the elements you need to feel safe and secure when there. All that truly matters is that it feels safe and loving. You have to start the loving sometime! After all, love is the end goal to all this work.

Once you have the space created, begin to add images that actually invoke a feeling of love for you. Animals or pets can often be very helpful in bringing in the feeling of love to your space. For some, invoking the feeling of love may be difficult, but don't let that stop you. You may be able to feel love for only a few seconds in the beginning, but it will grow if you keep exploring through your imagination what love looks and feels like to your heart. Your logical mind will not have the answer, since it always looks outside of itself for everything—not to mention that it most likely has a confused notion of love from past negative experiences. However, despite the bumps and bruises your heart has endured, it still remembers love. So keep playing with varying images till you feel something move within your heart.

Again, I want to stress that the point of all the work we will be doing is to allow ourselves to feel love coming from within. Self-love is not about seeking love from the outside. It is about reconnecting to the ever-present love that resides in all of our hearts. So don't worry if you have trouble in the beginning. Whether you believe it or not, you too have this wellspring of love inside of you, just waiting to be discovered.

My safe space started out years ago as a grove of giant ancient redwood trees that would shower me with flowers when I entered it. I felt so loved every time I arrived that I would run like a child and wrap my arms around one of the trees, which would in return wrap its branches around me like a giant mother's arms. I felt not only safe there but also loved and known. I used that image many times as a safe place to cry out my tears and fears. Those branches cradling me gave me great comfort and made me feel that I mattered. Even though I didn't understand why mattering was so important yet, what I did know was that it felt safe and loving.

Once you have created your space and filled it with as much safety and love as possible, allow yourself to just be within the space, feeling its effects on you and your heart. When you are done, you can end the meditation by thanking yourself for taking the time to do this work. You may not be able to *feel* gratitude for yourself at this early stage, but it will begin to set up a pattern of honoring yourself and the work you are willing to do.

Okay, put music on if you wish, get comfy, and close your eyes and create your safe, loving space.

FINAL THOUGHT

Now that you have created your safe place within, you can return to it anytime to do your work; but don't be surprised if it changes or suddenly reveals trails leading off in different directions. As you become more comfortable using your imagination, your subconscious and Higher Self will begin to show more inner areas for you to discover, heal, and transform, always for the purpose of learning about yourself so you can be empowered to choose love and return to your natural state of self-love. So stay flexible and let your inner landscape change and grow, but know you can always find your way back to this safe and loving space at any time.

Oh, and congrats to the first-timers. You just did your first working meditation. It doesn't matter how long you were able to stay there or how intricate or elaborate your inner world became. All that matters is that you tried.

If you had trouble keeping focused on images or were unable to feel any sense of love in the exercise, just know that that is okay. Remember: a major part of the journey toward self-love is getting to know yourself.

Rather than being disappointed, just note how your mind drifted and where it tended to drift to. Were there negative thoughts or voices trying to belittle the process? Did it feel as if it took forever when it actually was only a minute or two?

All of these responses will tell you a lot about what is going on inside you as well as how attached you are to following your ego's voice as the captain of the ship. It doesn't matter how adept you are at meditation. The point is to learn about yourself. As long as your intention remains focused on self-discovery, then you can consider it a success.

Your Homework

The homework for this chapter is very simple. Throughout the week, return to your safe space. See if you can stay there longer than before. Try expanding it with your imagination to make it even more loving and safe. How is it different if you use music or change the music? Observe whether you are able to feel the safety and love present in your space. Notice how you feel when you come out of meditation.

As always, end your meditation by thanking yourself for taking time to go inward. This may not seem like an important step, but you must remember that your goal is to return to self-love. These seemingly small gestures of love, gratitude, and respect will keep you focused on the end goal of receiving love from within.

If you don't bother to return to your safe space, ask yourself why. I am not going to preach that "you can only get out what you are willing to put in," because you already know that. The good news is that you can still discover much about yourself even if you don't do the homework. What excuse did you make for not doing it at least once? Was something or someone more important to you than you?

Not returning will tell you a lot about how you prioritize your needs or how easily you get distracted. Any information you garner about yourself in the end is always helpful. So don't berate yourself if you don't return; just acknowledge the true reason for it. Honesty—both mental and, especially, emotional—is key in making any changes in life.

During the week, if you catch yourself being judgmental about your meditations, imagination, or inability to *feel* love, silently say this affirmation:

I will be patient with myself.
I know my meditations are getting better and better.
I know I have a powerful imagination.
And I know I will feel love.

This action will aid you in consciously observing your life and detecting what is going on both inside you and around you rather than blindly going through your day. It will also set your intention on discovering your inner world and staying open to where that journey will take you, as well as reinforcing the end goal of feeling love.

NOTES

Chapter 2

What is a "Higher Self"?

Your Higher Self is the part of you that has never forgotten it is one with the divine and carries with it all the knowledge and power of that love.

It doesn't matter who you are or what you have done; you have a Higher Self. This Higher Self was with you before you were born and will be with you when you die and cross over. Many of us might have forgotten our Higher Selves, but that does not mean they are not alive within us. Your Higher Self is the part of you that *can* see the forest and the trees simultaneously and is nudging you forward down the most lovingly appropriate path for your growth in love.

Your Higher Self is that sudden inner urge that causes you to go left this time instead of right. It's that fleeting feeling that maybe you shouldn't do what you are getting ready to do because it is not in your best interest. It can be an inexplicable sense of peace that all will be all right as everything around you is falling apart.

Your Higher Self is always with you, whether you acknowledge it or not, constantly nudging you toward your greatest version of yourself. Simply put, your Higher Self *is* the wisest version of yourself because it is still connected and intimate with the divine.

The Higher Self knows you are deserving of your own love and is always presenting you with opportunities to reconnect to that truth. It is the part of you that knows your grandeur even when all you feel is small and insignificant. It is the part of you that, no matter how hard you try to forget, will remind you that you are never alone. It is the part of you that is continuously connected to the universe through love and is reminding you to have trust and faith in that love and yourself.

Your Higher Self will never shame you, scold you, or demean you. It never shouts but rather whispers gently into your ear. It never pushes you, always respecting your free will. It will simply nudge you with a thought or a feeling, allowing you to decide whether to listen or not. It is the part of you that cradles your dashed dreams, patiently waiting for you to pick yourself up and try again. It is pure *unconditional* love aligned with higher wisdom.

Your Higher Self is your navigator through this life. It is equipped with a roadmap and a 360-degree view of the terrain. It is intimate with everything you have gone through and with all that you have felt, for as you have felt your disappointments and pain, so too has your Higher Self felt it. Because it knows who you are—, a powerful being who has just temporarily forgotten his or her power—it will never force itself on you. However, if you choose to have a relationship with this part of yourself, it will become much more active in your life.

In truth, you actually will connect to this Higher Self when you lovingly work with your orphaned parts. It is this part of you that, despite the pain you feel, is still able to offer love and compassion to your various wounded orphans. You may even find yourself wondering, when doing this work, how you can offer such loving thoughts and words even though you never experienced that type of love or kind words in your outer life. That is your Higher Self at work.

There have been times when I was working with one of my orphans, trying to get her to understand her worth or value both to me and to the universe, when suddenly I found just the right words to crack open her heart. That was my Higher Self at work.

It is also your Higher Self that you will go to for your own healing and loving. Often before working with an inner orphan, I would need some loving for my present-day self. I discovered that if I was going to work to get one of my orphans to open up a bit more to feeling valued, I needed to also open up to feeling that value as well. So I would use my Higher Self to aid me just as I was going to aid my inner orphans. I would imagine her offering that love and wisdom in a way that would cause my heart to open up to feeling valued.

To speed up the healing work and to truly lock the new truth in your heart, you need to receive whatever love or wisdom you have just offered, or will offer, to your inner orphan. That is why I included taking time to receive love for yourself after any working meditations. What you offer to your orphans, you most likely will need also. Your Higher Self not only will help you with your orphaned parts by helping you to find the right words or actions but also will offer that same love and wisdom to you—if you will allow it.

I want to take a moment to mention something important here. When you open up to your inner orphans in the third part and begin to allow them to express their pain, it can actually feel very exhilarating. There is a sense of freedom and even lightness that comes from voicing what you have repressed. It can be very easy to end your meditations there because that venting has made you feel somewhat better. However, just venting your emotions is not leading you to any kind of permanent transformation. It is like putting a small bandage on a huge open wound. You may feel better in the moment, but nothing has truly changed. Lasting changes happen only through working with love.

So don't lose focus on the end goal of replacing that pain with love. It can feel very satisfying to release a big ball of pain you have been carrying. But don't let that sense of satisfaction keep you from replacing that pain with love.

I am going to repeat again that you should always take time to receive love during and at the end of your meditations, as this is where the transformation happens. This is where working with your Higher Self becomes so important. Your Higher Self is always ready to shower you with love in whatever form you need. Whether it is nurturing, peace, comfort, or even a sense of celebration, your Higher Self will use your imagination to offer you the love you need.

Your Higher Self is always present to hear your fears, wipe your tears, and offer a more expanding and loving viewpoint. There have been many times when I was stuck in some form of negative thinking, belief, or fear loop (unable to see the forest for the trees) and I went within and connected to this part of myself. Before I knew it, I was not only out of the fear loop, thanks to her nurturing, but I also had a much more loving and wise perspective on the situation.

There is a part of you that has never forgotten its connection to the divine and its own divinity. So why not reconnect with it? It will make your inner homework much easier, and you will have a wise and loving counselor at your beck and call for the rest of your life.

Having said all that, I know some will say, "*I don't need a Higher Self for love, wisdom, or guidance. I have Jesus [or Buddha, or angels] to do that for me.*" And that's great. I am not suggesting you replace your religious figures. One does not cancel out the other. We need all the love and wisdom possible. I personally have many guides and angels I have worked with through the years, but it is my Higher Self that taught me about love and showed me how to love myself.

What I want you to understand is that on the journey back to self-love, you have the opportunity to discover that you have a direct line to all the love and wisdom you will ever need right inside of you. Part of self-love is recognizing that the power is not outside of you. It never was. The power is you! You have everything you will ever need already inside of you, just waiting to be revealed.

Your Higher Self is the ultimate proof that you are loved. You were not dropped into this world unprepared. You were dropped into this world fully equipped with love and wisdom, and a powerful ally within to guide you forward on your chosen path.

When working on resurrecting or expanding your self-love, it may be helpful to remember the times you felt watched over or guided to take action that was not typical for you, or when you simply had a feeling that you needed to be kinder to yourself. Those are times when the Higher Self broke through your walls and revealed just how cherished you are.

QUESTIONS TO INVESTIGATE

1) Can you believe that there is a part of you always connected to a higher wisdom and love?

_____

_____

_____

_____

2) Do you believe some were given a better connection than you? If so, why?

_____

_____

_____

_____

3) Can you remember a time when you were internally prompted to do something?

_____

_____

_____

_____

4) Can you remember a time that you felt watched over for no apparent reason?

_____

_____

_____

_____

5) Have you ever suddenly found a solution to a problem or situation that just seemed to drop into your lap?

_____

_____

_____

_____

6) Do you believe you have a Higher Self? If not, why not?

_____

_____

_____

_____

7) Do you believe everyone has a Higher Self? If not, why not?

_____

_____

_____

_____

8) Have you ever noticed or paid attention to those whispers or inklings that come from within?

_____

_____

_____

_____

9) Can you remember a time you did pay attention and it worked out better than you could have imagined? Describe the situation.

_____

_____

_____

_____

10) Can you remember a time you didn't pay attention and you later wished you had? Describe the situation.

_____

_____

_____

_____

11) Can you believe the universe cherishes you? If not, why not?

_____

_____

_____

_____

12) What do you believe would happen if you chose to believe you were cherished?

_____

_____

_____

_____

13) Can you believe that much like a mother making sure her child has what she needs for the day, the universe is going to make sure you have what you need on this earthly journey? If not, why not?

_____

_____

_____

_____

14) Does the idea that you have this inner connection and power frighten you?

_____

_____

_____

_____

15) What would you have to give up if you knew you had a Higher Self always available?

_____

_____

_____

_____

16) Would anyone in your life be upset if you chose to believe you had a Higher Self? If so, who and why?

_____

_____

_____

_____

17) Who would you piss off by taking back your power and looking inward to your Higher Self instead of outward for love and wisdom?

_____

_____

_____

_____

18) How would your life change if you gave up the idea that you are powerless and acknowledged this divine part of yourself?

_____

_____

_____

_____

MEDITATION EXERCISE

Go into your safe space and call in your Higher Self, letting she or he know you want a more intimate relationship. Then begin to imagine this unconditional love and wisdom actualizing in front of you. Maybe you see a full body coming toward you, radiating light. Perhaps you *feel* a gentle, loving breeze sweep across your body and face. Possibly you are able to visualize the most beautiful eyes looking deeply into yours with loving recognition. It really doesn't matter what the image is. The image is just a way for you to connect. The images will change as you change. The Higher Self connection is all about love, so don't get stuck on an image. The images are just a way to invoke that connection and a feeling of love.

Before you say, "I can't do it," just know that if you were able to imagine a safe space, you can certainly use your imagination to visualize what this powerful all-loving part of you looks, and most importantly *feels*, like. Start by making it up. Don't sit in your safe space, waiting for something to happen. This holds true for all the meditative work. You are not waiting for something to appear or listening for some voice outside of yourself.

You are actively creating what you need. As I have said before, use your divine gift of imagination.

Imagine how an unconditional love would make itself known to you. And before you shout, "I have no idea what unconditional love even is," I want to remind you that you have read enough books and seen enough movies to have an inkling of what love could look like, even if you have never experienced it. For those who have pets, you know how you smother them with love when you return home for the night; wouldn't your Higher Self feel the same way about you? Use your imagination.

In the very early days of working with my Higher Self, all I could imagine was a breeze moving gently across my face like a caress. It didn't last long, but in those few seconds I was able to feel her love for me. While the feeling was small, it was the beginning of our conscious relationship. Through the years, the images have changed many times, depending on what my needs were, but the feeling of love has not. It has simply grown and expanded.

The point is to begin to make *real* for yourself that there is this powerful, loving, wise part of you who is constantly connected with you and who loves you beyond measure. Just because you have turned down the volume on your Higher Self's transmissions doesn't mean they are not still being broadcast. This exercise is to get you to turn up the volume and tune into the love that is you by connecting through your imagination.

It is all about the feelings and emotions this divine part of you invokes. How does it love you? Does it kiss your face all over? Does it run and hug you? Do its eyes light up when it sees you? How would a powerful all-loving part of you treat you? Keep imagining till you are able to *feel* its love, even if it is just for five seconds.

It doesn't matter how this love manifests; it matters only that you plug into it. If you hear anything negative or unloving, just know you have tapped into your negative ego, take a breath, and continue imaging the embodiment of unconditional love that is you.

When you are able to tap into your Higher Self's love, you will shed some tears at the reunion. I call these bittersweet tears because while you are crying tears of joy for having found your Higher Self, you are also crying tears of pain because you are now aware of how much you have missed this loving and wise part of you.

If it is hard to connect or to imagine this part of you, keep trying. Use the time to keep exploring what that kind of love might look and *feel* like. You will find that connection with practice if you stay focused on the energy of love.

When you are done, thank your Higher Self for its love. Let it know again that you want a more intimate relationship and that you want to let her or his love into your heart. Then thank yourself for doing the work.

Okay, put music on if you wish, get comfy, and close your eyes and meet your Higher Self. It has been waiting for you!

FINAL THOUGHT

While we all may start out in this world in very different situations, some with more and many with less, we all have been readied by the loving universe for the journey before us. Through our connection to our Higher Selves, we all are offered love, guidance, and wise counsel gently pushing us toward the most loving expressions of our beings. Our job is to pay attention and listen.

As you grow in trust with this part of yourself, ask it to be with you in all your meditations. Ask for its guidance in all that you do. Your Higher Self will offer you comfort as you begin to explore and connect with your emotions. The emotions you will be uncovering and working with can at times be overwhelming and even frightening. This important emotional work will be made much easier when you feel you have a beloved companion holding your hand and walking with you through the metaphorical fire.

When you are working on healing and integrating an orphaned part of yourself, include your Higher Self by inviting it into the work. Just as your orphans look to you for healing, love, and guidance, you can look to your Higher Self for the same.

The process of getting to know your Higher Self is actually the process of redefining what love is and how love feels when you allow it to touch your heart. Your Higher Self will teach you about love and the power of love. This is as important to your return to self-love as the healing of your orphans. So relish the time you spend getting to know your Higher Self, because it is through this reunion that you will learn the truth about love and the truth about yourself.

Needless to say, the relationship you form with your Higher Self will be the most impactful relationship you will experience in this life. Not only will she or he aid you in healing and integrating your orphans, enabling you to reclaim your self-love, but it will also become a vital partner in creating your new life based on that self-love.

Don't let this love and guidance fall on deaf ears. And know that no matter how hard you try to ignore your Higher Self, it will always be with you, patiently guiding and coaxing you toward your greatest good, even if you refuse to listen.

Your Homework

Take notice throughout your week of where and how many times you look outside of yourself for love and guidance in your daily life. Who or what do you feel has more power, knowledge, and love than you? Observe what you watch, read, or see online that reinforces your belief that you are powerless and must look outside of yourself for everything.

Look for the times when you suddenly know the answer to a question or how to suddenly resolve a problem or out of the blue feel loved for no specific reason. Then take a moment and thank your Higher Self, for you have just witnessed it in action.

Return to your safe space, and keep working to connect with your Higher Self. Does she or he appear to be so much more than you that it is unapproachable? Can you imagine it as an equal rather than a deity that is above you? Does it have a sense of humor? If you have one, believe me, so does your Higher Self.

You can ask your Higher Self if it has anything to say to you. You may at first hear a bunch of ego chatter, but eventually you will hear a word or small phrase, or you may even see an image or symbol that feels different because it goes right into your heart.

Perhaps your Higher Self brings you a gift. Imagine what that gift might be. You will know when it is your Higher Self presenting the gift and not your ego because anything coming from your Higher Self will touch your heart. Remember: your heart will always be your best barometer as to whether you are dealing with your ego or your Higher Self.

If you have a lousy day, try laying your head in your Higher Self's lap and telling it all about it. Imagine its loving response. If you have fear, allow your Higher Self to take it from you and envelop you in a loving embrace. If you feel unloved, allow your Higher Self to touch your heart with its hand. If you need to cry, allow your Higher Self to hold you as you cry. Let your Higher Self love you in any form that feels good to you.

Keep using your imagination as a way to connect. Remember: whatever you imagine is coming from you. And since your Higher Self is you, your imagination is a perfect conduit for communication. As long as it is unconditional love, you are connecting.

During your day, when you witness yourself feeling powerless, inept, or alone, take a deep breath and silently say the following affirmation:

I have everything I will ever need for
my journey already inside of me.
I have a Higher Self who knows me
and loves me and is guiding me
at all times;
that is how much the universe loves me.
Thank you.

This action will aid you in consciously observing your life and detecting what is going on around you rather than blindly going through your day. It will set your intention on claiming your power through your love and connection with your Higher Self. It will also remind you that you are fully capable of handling whatever life puts in front of you.

NOTES

Chapter 3

Why are emotions so important for returning to self-love?

Self-love is rooted in the heart. You must know how to work through your feelings to rediscover the emotions of self-love; otherwise, it is just mental masturbation.

I have met many people who will do anything not to feel those bad or dark feelings, and it is not just the people who you can see numb themselves from their feelings. It is so called enlightened people as well. They honor the light but run from the dark. The problem with that is that we are beings who have both light and dark aspects. To deny the dark aspects of ourselves is to cut ourselves off from our wholeness. In truth, just because you deny or ignore something does not make it go away. That suppressed emotion or feeling will struggle to be recognized, and the more it struggles to come to the surface, the more energy you have to use to shove it back down. Then you will find you have focused almost all of your emotional energy on keeping the dark away, leaving yourself emotionally unavailable for joy. You may think you are avoiding pain, but you are also avoiding joy. If you want to feel the joy and happiness of being alive, you must also risk feeling the agony and pain of life.[1]

Emotional awareness is vital for self-mastery. Without emotional awareness, you cannot work with or master the other lessons of life. You must know what you are feeling and why you are feeling it in order to make new choices that will enable you to feel and experience something different. Your emotions are your best navigational tool for the simple reason that while your head may lie to you, your emotions never do. They

---

[1] McClung, J., *How Learning to Say Goodbye Taught Me How to Live* (Bloomington, Indiana: Balboa Press, 2015), 3.

will always tell you whether what you believe about yourself or a situation is helpful or harmful. You get a knot in your stomach when someone is degrading you because you know deep down that what that person is saying is a lie. However, if you ignore that feeling (that signal from your emotional body), you will most likely unconsciously believe it or create new beliefs around the situation, such as "people are just out to get me."

Another reason to make friends with your emotional body is that you will need to feel your wounds to heal them. Your core wounds, which created your viewpoint of yourself and the world around you, must be healed through feeling as well as understanding. You cannot just think your way out of it. When you change a viewpoint or belief, it must be anchored in the heart. Often, to make room for the new belief, you must clear the old emotion out of the way.

> Our emotions are meant to act as a sophisticated guidance system, allowing us to know when something is off or out of balance. If someone or something triggers you, rather than wasting your time being angry over the trigger, see it as an alert that something within needs attention. It may be that you need healing on some core issues and wounds or that you have beliefs that need to change. Or it could be an indication that what is happening is not in your best interest and that action is required. Remember, you would not have an emotional reaction if some inner part of you were not activated. Your job is to be the detective and to follow those emotions to their core where

the real transformational work is accomplished. Don't run from your emotions but rather honor their importance as a very integral tool for navigating your way through life.[2]

Your emotions are a wonderful gift and are part of your spiritual toolbox for creating. Your emotions, along with your beliefs, create your experiences, and yet so few truly understand how to work with their emotional bodies. Most of us were never taught how to maneuver through our personal emotional worlds. Instead of understanding our emotions, we often were told which emotions were appropriate and which were to be avoided at all costs. Suppressing an emotion doesn't work. I think that is what makes it so difficult to return to the emotional work.

The emotional body has been stuffed with so many unexpressed emotions that it can feel overwhelming to even begin. It is as if we are afraid what will happen if we actually allow ourselves to feel our emotions. Will we explode? Will we become angry lunatics—or worse, murderers—if we feel our rage? No! The goal is not to feed the emotion, which I believe suppressing it actually does on an unconscious level, but to allow it to move up and out of our physical bodies. The quickest way to move through an emotion is to express it and replace it with more loving emotions. This healthy expression of an emotion will begin to dissipate its power. To repress

---

[2] McClung, J., *How Learning to Say Goodbye Taught Me How to Live*, 3.

an emotion is the quickest way to be tied to it. Don't be afraid. No expressed emotion is going to kill you. I cannot say the same for an unexpressed emotion.

First off, you are going to find a safe place where you can be alone and feel emotions and follow them to their sources. Remember: there are emotions underneath the surface emotion. You may think you are just mad at a friend, but I guarantee there is more going on than anger. Perhaps you are hurt or sad. Perhaps your anger is masking a fear or a feeling of guilt or shame. Or perhaps your friend's actions triggered or awoke a childhood wound. Those are the energies you would want to work on. Why am I hurt? What do I fear? Am I afraid she knows I am not trustworthy? Am I sad because I knew she would quit liking me? Follow the train where it takes you.

You will discover that underneath the phrase is a lie you have been telling yourself for years, such as "Nobody ever loves me." That is the issue that needs healing. Just because you don't want to own a feeling does not mean it will stop being part of your reality. It *will* find a way to be heard—if not through you, then through others acting as shadow mirrors of what you are avoiding within yourself.

Have you ever noticed that people who have unresolved anger seem to attract angry situations? Isn't it better to discover and express a feeling in the comfort of your private safe space rather than allowing your unconscious to create the same drama over and over again until you release the energy? Remember to be compassionate with yourself as you begin to awaken to your emotional body. To allow oneself to finally feel can be unsettling for many, depending on where they fit on the spectrum of emotional types.

I believe there are two extreme emotional types at the opposite ends of the spectrum: the explosive type, who vomits every emotion he or she has on whomever is nearby, and the pretender, who shoves every emotion as far down as possible and acts as if nothing ever fazes him or her. I think we all fit somewhere within that sliding scale at different times in our lives until we find balance.

Explosive types may find it easy to connect with their emotions. However, the trick for them may be that while they are very aware that they feel, they are rarely able to go underneath the surface emotions to their true feelings of pain and take responsibility for those feelings. Somehow they believe the way they feel is everyone else's fault, and they usually make everyone around them pay for it. They are constantly feeding their emotion rather than healthily expressing it privately and then dissipating it by moving into more loving feelings.

Explosive types will tend to skip the loving part of a meditation process because the sense of relief and even the false sense of power they receive through venting their feelings is enough. It is what they have grown accustomed to in their outer-world expressions, so they treat their inner world the same. For them, getting into their emotional body won't be difficult. Understanding that they feel that way because there is something *inside* of them that needs attention and that they can choose more loving emotions will take practice.

Pretenders are those people who have become pros at suppressing their emotions. They have become quite adept at pretending things don't bother them. They compartmentalize their feelings in order to maintain the status quo. A pretender could have a brutal fight with someone, but in order to keep that relationship, he or she might shove his or her anger or hurt down and pretend it was no big deal, or he or she might make excuses as to why it happened.

Pretenders are also quite good at being passive-aggressive, often with no knowledge they are doing so. These people will have the hardest time connecting to their emotional bodies, because they have decided which emotions are safe and which ones are not. For them to tap into unexpressed anger, rage, hurt, or shame will take practice. They fear what will happen if they feel all that is within them.

Both of the types mentioned above deny their true emotions. Spewing keeps one from taking responsibility for one's life and takes away any opportunity to improve or change one's life, while pretending sucks the life out of a person and keeps her or him from living an authentic, emotionally rich life.

The bottom line is that we were gifted with emotions not to run from them or to use them as weapons. Emotions are a vital tool for creating and experiencing the world around us. So get comfortable with your emotions. They will tell you much about your pain but also much about your beauty.

As you work with the following questions, try to *feel* your way through each one. Which question makes you nervous? Which question makes you mad? Which question do you immediately reject as silly or not pertaining to you? All of this will be a clue as to where you need to work.

The goal is to become comfortable with all emotions. I would like to remind you again that working with your emotions is a private affair. It is not to give you a license to dump your emotions on another. Determining what you feel, and more importantly *why you feel it*, is your homework. So do it in private!

QUESTIONS TO INVESTIGATE

(Be as specific and as detailed as you can be.)

1) What negative emotion are you carrying around?

_____

_____

_____

_____

2) Do you have hidden pockets of resentment and blame?

_____

_____

_____

_____

3) Are you at times jealous or envious of others?

_____

_____

_____

_____

4) Do you remember past hurts or hold grudges?

_____
_____
_____
_____

5) Are you carrying around shame about what you have experienced or done?

_____
_____
_____
_____

6) Do you have sadness or hopeless feelings about how your life has turned out thus far?

_____
_____
_____
_____

7) Are you secretively angry with people or the world?

_____
_____
_____
_____

8) Do you feel life has been unfair to you? If so, why?

_____
_____
_____
_____

9) If you are feeling a negative emotion, do you own it or blame someone else for it?

_____

_____

_____

_____

10) Do you often say, "Well, they made me feel that way"?

_____

_____

_____

_____

11) Do you believe that if others would just change their behavior, you would feel better?

_____

_____

_____

_____

12) Do you immediately react when emotionally triggered by someone's words or actions?

_____

_____

_____

_____

13) How has that kind of reaction impacted your life?

_____

_____

_____

_____

14) Have you ever looked within to see why you are having such strong reactions?

_____

_____

_____

_____

15) Have you ever discovered later that your reaction had nothing to do with the other person or situation but everything to do with you?

_____

_____

_____

_____

16) Have you ever been honest and owned that something inside of you got triggered, or is it *always* about the other person?

_____

_____

_____

_____

17) Have you noticed that the same emotional triggers appear again and again, and what are those triggers?

_____

_____

_____

_____

18) Have you ever considered that it might be you creating these situations, and what would it mean to you if you did discover you had a hand in creating the situations?

_____

_____

_____

_____

19) What emotion do you avoid at all costs? Why?

_____

_____

_____

_____

20) How comfortable are you feeling anger or sadness or disappointment?

_____

_____

_____

_____

21) Do you allow yourself to feel these emotions, or do you quickly tell yourself not to feel that way?

_____

_____

_____

_____

22) Can you admit to yourself when you are feeling jealous or envious of others' good fortune, and how does it make you *feel?*

_____

_____

_____

_____

23) When hit with hopelessness or despair, do you pretend everything is okay? If so, why do you do that?

_____

_____

_____

_____

24) What happens when something good happens to you? What is your first reaction or thought?

_____

_____

_____

_____

25) What would happen if you allowed yourself to feel joy or pride over an achievement?

_____

_____

_____

_____

26) Do you judge your emotions?

_____

_____

_____

_____

27) What emotion do you feel is absolutely despicable?

_____

_____

_____

_____

28) What do you do if you find yourself feeling the emotion you listed above?

_____

_____

_____

_____

29) What is the difference between "positive" emotions and "negative" emotions?

_____

_____

_____

_____

30) Are "negative" emotions necessarily bad for you?

_____

_____

_____

_____

31) Have you ever considered that "negative" emotions are just a warning system?

_____

_____

_____

_____

32) Are some emotions only for the weak and other emotions only for the strong?

_____

_____

_____

_____

33) Do you think crying is okay, or is it just for the young or weak?

_____

_____

_____

_____

34) When is the last time you allowed yourself to cry? Why?

_____

_____

_____

_____

35) Do you have a safe, place to vent your emotions alone, or do you just dump them wherever you are?

_____

_____

_____

_____

36) Do you believe checking in on your emotions is a waste of time?

_____

_____

_____

_____

37) Do you prefer to suck it up and get on with what is "really important"? Why?

_____

_____

_____

_____

38) Do you think strong people don't need to do emotional work?

_____

_____

_____

_____

39) Do you think it is selfish to take time for yourself?

_____

_____

_____

_____

40) Do you see emotions as weak or as something to be controlled?

_____

_____

_____

_____

41) How has the above belief worked for you?

_____

_____

_____

_____

42) Who mirrored that behavior for you?

_____

_____

_____

_____

43) Did it really seem to work for that person?

_____

_____

_____

_____

44) Did that behavior add much joy and excitement to his or her life?

_____

_____

_____

_____

45) If not, then why are you carrying that behavior forward in your life? What do you get out of it?

_____

_____

_____

_____

46) If you knew emotions were an integral part of navigating and creating your life, would you look at emotions differently?

_____

_____

_____

_____

47) Were you shamed for certain emotions?

_____

_____

_____

_____

48) Which emotions are "shameful"?

_____

_____

_____

_____

49) What would you do with these emotions if and when you felt them?

_____

_____

_____

_____

50) Were certain emotions off limits because of your gender or culture?

_____

_____

_____

_____

51) What would happen if you admitted you had these emotions?

_____

_____

_____

_____

52) Who would you disappoint if you admitted you had these emotions?

_____

_____

_____

_____

53) What does that say about those that do exhibit such emotions?

_____

_____

_____

_____

54) Why are these emotions forbidden to begin with?

_____
_____
_____
_____

55) Who taught you to feel shame about your feelings or emotions?

_____
_____
_____
_____

56) What would change in your life if you quit denying your emotions?

_____
_____
_____
_____

57) What do you fear you would lose if you quit denying your emotions?

_____
_____
_____
_____

58) Who would you upset by changing?

_____

_____

_____

_____

59) What relationship would stop "working" if you were honest with yourself about your emotions?

_____

_____

_____

_____

60) What lie would you have to let go of if you honestly owned your feelings?

_____

_____

_____

_____

61) If you became adept at understanding your feelings, how do you think that would change the way you move through the world?

_____

_____

_____

_____

MEDITATION EXERCISE

Invite your Higher Self to join you, and begin your meditation by envisioning your emotional body. It can be at the center of your safe space, or perhaps it is in a cave off to the side, lying on a slab of rock like mine was when I first found it. Wherever your imagination takes you, see it as a separate body lying in front of you. Yes, some of you may feel as if you are just making it up, but that's okay. In a sense, you *are* making it up. However, remember that what you are imagining is still coming from you. Eventually, with practice, you will be comfortable with your gift of imagination and will begin to trust what it brings forth. For now, just work to the best of your ability to envision your emotional body.

What does it look like? Is it large or small? Does it appear young or old? What colors radiate from it? Is it vibrant or dull? Does it look like you, or does it look like a stranger? Is it full of wounds, lying on a sick bed? If so, do you feel compelled to nurse it and love it, or are you repelled by its "weakness"? Imagine the body as clearly as possible. Try touching different places on the body. What emotions are trapped in the head, the heart, the arms, or the back of your emotional body? See if you can feel the pain that is locked within it when you touch it. How does it react to your touch? If it has gone numb or seems to be dead, how does that realization make you *feel?* Does it make you sad or angry that you have unwittingly ignored this vital part of your being? What you see and feel, and your reactions to it, will tell you a lot about your relationship to your emotions.

Stay with the image as long as you can, feeling what it is willing to share with you. You can even ask your emotional body if it has something it wants to tell you. It may answer with words, but most likely the communication will be through emotions, since emotions are its natural form of communication. So pay attention to what you are feeling as you get to know your emotional body. This is an exercise of feeling, so no matter what you imagine, you will shed some tears. And if you don't shed some tears, don't worry. It just means it will take some practice for you to open up to your emotional side.

When you are done exploring, take a moment to send your emotional body some love and thank it for bring an essential part of your being. If you can't *feel* love at this time, then gently stroke it or kiss it. The point is to let it know you care.

Then have your Higher Self offer love and nurturing to your emotional body. Imagine how it touches and interacts with this part of your being. Perhaps your Higher Self calls in angels (or whatever image of love works for you) to surround your emotional body and care for it till you return. Observe unconditional love in action.

Back in the day when I was working to connect to my emotions, at the end of my meditation I would lie next to my emotional body, holding its hand, as my Higher Self showered us both in healing light. Imagine and do what feels the most loving and most appropriate for you and your emotional body.

Once you are done offering love to your emotional body, take a few moments to receive love for you. Again use your imagination. Perhaps your Higher Self has you lie down in a stream, with beautiful water gently flowing over you. Maybe you have beautiful lights or an angel envelop you in love. A beloved pet can appear, covering your face with wet kisses. Or, as in my early meditations, a tree can embrace you with nurturing love. The image of love doesn't matter. All that matters is that you create a loving moment for yourself.

You might be very surprised at what your imagination and your Higher Self bring forward. And much like your safe space, the images of love will change and grow as you become more comfortable with allowing your imagination to guide you.

Once you have allowed yourself to be loved, thank yourself for taking the time to do this work, and thank your Higher Self for its love and help.

Okay, put music on if you wish, get comfy, and close your eyes and meet your emotional body.

Final Thought

It is not a mistake that we are emotional beings. The mistake is that we were never taught how to honor and work with our emotions. The good news is that it is never too late to learn how to work with your emotional body and heal the wounds that are stuck within it.

You can spend all your life working to change your mind, but if you are unwilling to change your heart, you will be spinning your wheels. You must be willing to *feel* to make lasting changes. I know it can be quite scary to feel—especially if you have become adept at not acknowledging that you have any feelings to begin with! But the only way you will change your outer experiences is to acknowledge truthfully what you feel inwardly, and more importantly *why* you feel it. Only then can you consciously begin to heal past wounds, change the toxic beliefs born out of those wounds, and return to self-love.

You then will be free to use your emotions as the navigational system they were meant to be, allowing you to choose love over fear moment by moment.

YOUR HOMEWORK

If you are a pretender with emotions, take notice throughout your week of where and how many times you ignore your emotions. Do you ignore them or shove them down when people you like or need are involved? What about people you don't like or need—how do you handle your emotions around them?

If you are an explosive type, what causes you to explode your emotions on those around you? Take notice of how often you dump your emotions on others. How does this affect those around you? How does it affect you?

If you have an emotional reaction during the day, return to your emotional body in meditation and allow it to vent the emotions and feelings fueling your reaction with your loving support. You may discover that while you felt anger in the situation, the emotional body felt fear. So listen as you would to a close friend. Just by the action of listening, you will begin to open up to what is really going on inside of you. Also, if you are the type who skips the receiving of love at the end of the meditation, make that one of your goals.

If you had trouble connecting to your emotional body, try again in meditation. Perhaps the image of a body doesn't work for you. If not, choose a different image. The image doesn't matter; the connection does. Keep trying. You will know when you have found an image that works for you because you will *feel* it! The whole point to all of this is to get to know your emotional side and to reconnect to it with love. If you are able to feel your emotions without the use of an image, that is perfect. Just use your safe space as a place to voice those emotions in privacy and to offer and receive love.

Pay attention to how certain emotions are valued or devalued in your thoughts and actions, in others around you, and in the things you read or watch on TV or online. When you witness emotions being devalued or ridiculed, reject the idea by declaring, "No, I will no longer judge my emotions." Then silently say the following affirmation:

I honor my gift of emotions.
I know my emotions are a vital part of my being
and an important tool for knowing myself.

This action will aid you in consciously observing your life and detecting what is going on around you rather than blindly going through your day. It will also set your intention on moving into owning the value of your emotions for healing, creating, and navigating the world around you.

NOTES

Part 2

The Three Components
of Self-Love

Chapter 4

What is self-love?

Self-love is the knowing in your heart that your very being is loveable, loving, and loved.

The truth about self-love is that it is the basis of everything you believe about yourself and the world around you and therefore is the basis of everything you will create and experience. I don't care how many affirmations you repeat, how many techniques you practice to create your reality, or how hard you work to achieve your goals or desires; without a healthy anchoring of self-love, you will be fighting an uphill battle. Your outer world will constantly find ways to mirror that lack of self-love in some form or another.

I have used the term "knowing in your heart" specifically because self-love must be rooted in the heart. It is not enough to walk around spouting your virtues or stating how fabulous you are. Unless self-love is rooted in your heart, you are simply playing a mind game with yourself. Trust me when I say that all mind games eventually turn around and bite you. In fact, I have often found that the people who appear the most self-confident or vocal about how they love themselves lack the truth of self-love.

Self-love is the understanding that while your ego personality may not be perfect, your being, or the core of who you are, is always lovable, loving, and loved. Without those three components rooted in your heart, you will feel as if you are somehow lacking.

We come into this world with all three of those truths anchored in our being. However, by early childhood we have begun to lose our connection to these truths. There is no shame in this. It is simply that as children we naturally look outside of ourselves to find out who we are and what our place is in the family and the world. There lies the rub! Too often, adults who are lacking in self-love are the ones guiding the children. So instead of expanding the child's sense of self-love, they constrict it with doubt, shame, and fear. Simply put, the child will often mirror the adult's own feelings of self-loathing. Then those same children grow up and repeat the same toxic behavior. To be fair, it is not only adults; siblings and friends can also have a hand in causing us to distance ourselves from the truth of who we are.

"Self-loathing" may feel like a strong word to use, but if you feel that you are missing one of the components of self-love, you will have an underlying feeling of self-loathing for not being loveable enough, not loving well enough, or not being valuable enough to merit being loved. Those lies will cause you to loathe your very being in some form or fashion.

Rediscovering self-love can be challenging for some for the simple reason that it takes a certain amount of insight and wisdom to acknowledge that we lack in self-love and to know how to remedy it. We have been taught to look outward for proof of our value, worth, and even the goodness of our love.

The problem with this is that you will never believe you are valuable or worthy if you do not believe it in your heart first. It does not matter how many people may try to tell you; you will not buy it. Oh, it may work for a while, but eventually you will sabotage yourself because you believe you do not deserve it. So you get back on the hamster wheel again and again, trying desperately to find that sense that you matter and are loved. You may think a job or person will fill the void, but neither ever does. Why? Because you are going at it backward.

One of the easiest ways to discover whether you are on that hamster wheel is to look at your behavior. Do you do things to please people even when you would rather not? Do you put others' needs before yours, often to your detriment? Do you berate yourself for supposed mistakes you may have made? Do you allow others to treat you badly? Do you live as a martyr, trying to prove your worth by what you do and hoping that if you sacrifice enough you will be rewarded with what you feel is missing? All of these traits indicate a need to go inward, not outward, to find the way back to self-love.

Another indication of the lack of self-love is blaming or bullying. If you are constantly looking to blame others for what you feel inside or for what is missing on the outside, realize that there is a false premise at work here: that you somehow are not as important to the universe as another and that others have power over you. You believe that you are powerless and therefore a victim. The other side of that coin is the bully. The bully has the victim energy just as the person who blames, but the bully acts out that sense of powerlessness or being unlovable by trying to gain power and control over others. All of these actions stem from the lack of self-love.

When you have self-love, you have no need to prove your worthiness, your value, or your superiority over others. You no longer look for the outer world to prove your worth. You already know it in your heart. Your self-love tells you so. You must discover *inwardly* the beauty, value, and worth that inherently define you.

The fact is, no one can give you what you refuse to give to yourself. Most times this means rolling up your sleeves and doing the hard work of healing your past wounds and changing the negative beliefs (lies) that you created out of those wounds. You must be honest with yourself. That means removing your masks and defenses, working to let go of all of your ego's safety nets and having the courage to stand in front your inner mirror of truth.

That idea can seem scary to a lot of people, which is why I think it often takes a loss or crisis to force us to look deeper within and to do the heavy lifting of transformation. However, if you are willing to do the work, you can find your way back to love and actually fall in love with yourself again. When you truly love yourself, you open yourself up to receiving as well as offering that love to others.

The power of knowing you are lovable, loving, and loved enables you to move through the world with an open heart and a mind free from judgments and thus the freedom to experience life with all of your being. Isn't that something worth going for?

Questions to Investigate

(Remember to be as detailed as possible)

1) How important is self-love to your life? Why?

_____

_____

_____

_____

2) Is working toward reclaiming your self-love selfish?

_____

_____

_____

_____

3) If so, who taught you that? How did that belief work
   for him or her?

_____

_____

_____

_____

4) How have you defined self-love in the past?

_____

_____

_____

_____

5) Does your definition of self-love have to do with actions only, such as what you will do and what you won't do?

_____

_____

_____

_____

6) Is your self-love contingent on how others see you or treat you?

_____

_____

_____

_____

7) Have you ever considered that self-love is your responsibility and has nothing to do with other people and how they see you?

_____

_____

_____

_____

8) Have you ever *felt* love for yourself? If yes, include what caused you to feel it and what the feeling of love felt like. If no, include how it makes you feel now to admit that.

_____

_____

_____

_____

9) Are you aware of what you really think about yourself?

_____

_____

_____

_____

10) Have you ever admitted to yourself that what you say and how you present yourself to the world are very different than what you *feel* about yourself on the inside, and what are those differences?

_____

_____

_____

_____

11) Do you believe self-love determines how you will experience the world? If not, what determines your experience?

_____

_____

_____

_____

12) Have you ever been the victim or bully, or both? What was your behavior in the situation?

_____

_____

_____

_____

13) What were you *feeling* about yourself when you were a victim or bully?

_____

_____

_____

_____

14) What do you hope to gain by reclaiming your self-love?

_____

_____

_____

_____

15) Who would be upset, or what would have to change, if you reclaimed your self-love?

_____

_____

_____

_____

16) How do you think your world would change if you loved yourself?

_____

_____

_____

_____

MEDITATION EXERCISE

Invite your Higher Self to join you and enter your safe space. Begin to explore your feelings around self-love or the lack of self-love. Use your safe space as your personal confessional, knowing you can express your truth with no judgment. Stand in that sacred space and reveal to your surroundings or your Higher Self how you feel about lacking in self-love. Does it make you sad or mad? Are you afraid when you think of loving yourself? Are you full of frustration because you don't know what you think or because you are unable to feel? Do you want to blame someone for not teaching you how to love yourself? This is the place to let all those feelings out and express them fully, with no holds barred. As I said, this is the place to confess all your thoughts and feelings that you so carefully hide from others and even yourself. Let it rip.

Also remember that this is about feeling, not logic, so don't edit or judge the feelings or thoughts that come up for you. Much like someone delivering a stream-of-consciousness speech, you want to allow every feeling and thought to flow into the next one, not worrying about whether or not it follows a rational line. This is where music is helpful. It is one of the best ways to move into that stream-of-consciousness energy.

Notice if admitting you are separated from your own love causes discomfort or shame. Is there a part of you that feels it is self-indulgent to focus on the self? Is there another part of you that feels you should just get over it? Do you hear internal voices telling you that you are not worthy or deserving of love, or that the problem is that you are just not good enough? Pay attention to everything that comes up as you explore your feelings. Allow those feelings to begin to expose your beliefs concerning self-love.

The more you know about what you feel and believe about self-love, the better equipped you will be to make the necessary changes within to reclaim your birthright of self-love. It is also perfectly acceptable to admit to yourself that you don't know anything about self-love. How does that revelation make you feel? How does it make you feel to know you have never considered it important to love yourself? If you are someone who doesn't know what he or she feels or thinks about self-love, then scream out to the heavens (in your mind, of course), "I don't know." The bottom line is that there are no right or wrong answers. All that is required is being as honest as you can with yourself.

Once you are done, take a deep breath and allow your Higher Self to offer you comfort and some nurturing. Stay with it until you can feel its kindness touch your heart.

Once you have allowed yourself to *feel* loved, you can end the meditation by thanking yourself for taking the time to do this work. Of course, thank your Higher Self as well.

Okay, put music on if you wish, get comfy, and close your eyes and explore your feelings around self-love.

Final Thought

Self-love is a state of being. We are such an action-oriented world that the idea of just *being* can be a hard concept for many. There is a sense that we must prove ourselves at all times. We can't just be rooted in self-love; we must prove it. While actions can and *will* be born out of that love, in truth, self-love requires no actions. It just is. And because it is an inner state that is constant, no outside force or situation can change it.

When you know in the bottom of your heart that you are lovable, loving, and loved, your time and energy will no longer be spent looking for love or safety in the outside world, for you will have discovered it where it always resided—within you. And with this revelation, a new sense of freedom will be your diving force to express the love that is you in everything you do and with everyone you meet.

YOUR HOMEWORK

Notice throughout your week when and how many times self-loathing is mirrored in your life either in your thoughts and actions or in those of others around you, as well as in what you read or watch on TV or online. Then use your safe space to explore what you discovered in your daily life concerning self-love. It is your sacred place to share your true feelings and thoughts, so use it. If something in your daily life really triggered your feelings of loathing, go to your safe space and vent your feelings freely. You will discover much just by listening to yourself. Keep pushing to go underneath your initial reaction and get to the lie you have believed about yourself and the world around you.

Next ask your Higher Self to offer new loving energies and images to replace the loathing ones you just vented. If you have just vented about how you are worthless and nobody will ever love you, it can be very powerful to have your Higher Self wrap its arms around you and hug you tightly like a devoted mother. Whatever image you choose, allow your Higher Self to demonstrate the truth: you are worthy of your own love.

Lastly, every time you notice self-loathing in yourself or others, immediately declare to yourself, "No, I reject that lie!" Then silently say the following affirmation:

I no longer choose to hate or degrade myself.
I am now choosing to learn to love myself.
I choose love always!

You may not know quite yet what that means, but you will be setting your intention to choose love over loathing, and it will keep you focused on your end goal of returning to self-love.

NOTES

Chapter 5

What does it mean to be lovable?

Being lovable means being worthy of love—period! There are no exemptions or exceptions.

The very fact that you exist means that you are worthy of love and therefore are lovable. I want to be clear here that I am not referring to whether your behavior is always lovable. Let's face it; some of our actions stemming from our lack of self-love are not particularly lovable. However; I am not talking about behaviors or actions. I am talking about your core being—not your personality traits or behaviors that were born out of loathing. Your core being is lovable. I repeat: Your core being is lovable. There is nothing in your makeup or how you were designed that makes you unlovable to the universe.

However, for many of us, this truth has been beaten out of us, either metaphorically or literally. We begin to see our lovability as something that is negotiated: "I will find you worthy of love if you do X, Y, and Z for me." Perhaps your lovability is contingent on someone else's mood for the day; one day you are worthy of love, and the next day that person can't stand the sight of you. Over time you begin to see your lovability as something to be bestowed onto you by outside forces, and that false notion will set you up for a lifetime of disappointment. There is nothing crazier than asking someone else who is most likely struggling with his or her own issues of self-loathing to prove to you that you are lovable. It is literally asking the blind to lead the blind!

You are worthy of love no matter who you are or what you have done. Just as a newborn baby is worthy of his or her mother's love, you are now and will always be worthy of the universe's love. Others' reactions to you

97

may have impacted your belief about your lovability, but in truth their reactions have more to do with them than you. Your worthiness of love has nothing to do with another person; nor do you need to have others confirm that worthiness. A person living alone on top of a mountain can be rooted in the truth that he or she is lovable, while a person surrounded by family and friends may secretly feel unlovable. It is not about who is in your life or how many people are around you. It is about what you know inside of you.

Self-love is about the self. For many people—especially women who have been trained to find their worthiness of love in relationship to others (e.g., a good wife or good mother)—this can be a hard truth to accept. But nonetheless it is true. Your worthiness of love must begin with the self. You cannot find your lovability through other people. It doesn't work. And the real paradox is that without your heart being rooted in the truth that you are worthy of love, you will never allow others' love for you fully into your heart.

If you can't believe in your own lovability, why do you think you will believe it any better simply because it is coming from another person? And what happens to your lovability if and when that person leaves your life? I am not saying it doesn't feel good to have others make you feel worthy of love, but it is a temporary fix. And just like an addict, you will be on the constant lookout for your next fix, thus being permanently beholden to your pusher of choice. I know it is comforting to the ego to have the world see that someone believes you are lovable. But none of these outside influences will fill up the hole you feel on the inside.

You want to have the truth of your lovability locked deep within your heart, never dependent on another. That is why many relationships (romantic or friendships) are codependent, with each person looking for proof of their lovability through the other. Healthy relationships have two people, each rooted in self-love, coming together to express that love in responsible partnership.

So if you want to experience your lovability, you must look within and find out what you believe about your lovability, and what is keeping you from living this truth.

QUESTIONS TO INVESTIGATE

1) Do you believe you are worthy of love? If not, why not?

_____

_____

_____

_____

2) Is your lovability dependent on what you do or how you act?

_____

_____

_____

_____

3) Do you believe your very presence can upset people or make them angry?

_____

_____

_____

_____

4) Do you blame yourself when others treat you badly or unfairly?

_____

_____

_____

_____

5) Do you look for others to confirm that you are lovable and how is that achieved?

_____

_____

_____

_____

6) Do you need constant attention or compliments to feel better about yourself?

_____

_____

_____

_____

7) How do you talk to yourself when something goes wrong in your life?

_____

_____

_____

_____

8) Do you allow others to treat you badly with no consequences? If so, why?

_____

_____

_____

_____

9) Do you rate your lovability by how many people are in your life or friend you on Facebook?

_____

_____

_____

_____

10) From whom did you pick up the lie that you are not worthy of love?

_____

_____

_____

_____

11) Can you even consider that this person was wrong and perhaps had no idea what he or she was talking about?

_____

_____

_____

_____

12) Why did you believe this person?

_____

_____

_____

_____

13) Does the idea that this person was wrong scare you
or trouble you in any way?

_____

_____

_____

_____

14) Do you believe it is okay or safe to believe you are
worthy of love?

_____

_____

_____

_____

15) Have you ever felt that you must earn love?

_____

_____

_____

_____

16) Can you believe that every single person is worthy of love? If not, why not?

_____

_____

_____

_____

17) What would have to change in your life if you knew you were worthy of love?

_____

_____

_____

_____

18) Who would be upset if you chose to believe you were lovable, just as you are, in the universe's eyes?

_____

_____

_____

_____

19) What do you believe is the biggest obstacle keeping you from knowing and *feeling* that you are worthy of love?

_____

_____

_____

_____

20) How would you move through the world differently
   if you knew you were worthy of love at all times?

_____

_____

_____

_____

MEDITATION EXERCISE

Enter your safe space with your Higher Self, and begin to explore your feelings concerning your worthiness of love. Use your safe space as your personal confessional, knowing you can express your truth with no judgment. Stand in that sacred space and reveal to your surroundings or your Higher Self how you feel about not feeling worthy of love.

How hard is it for you to believe that you, as well every single person alive, are worthy of love? Be honest with yourself if you feel some people are more worthy or if you feel you are more worthy than others. Have people close to you recognized your lovability, or have they made you do something to earn it? How has that made you feel? Did your parents know they were worthy of love? You want to look underneath every rock to find out where you came up with the belief that you are not lovable.

Look at how your family treated the idea of your worthiness. Was it given or taken away depending on their mood? Does your religion support the idea that everyone is worthy of love, or must something be done to receive it? Look at your childhood, your friends, and your partners, and as you do so, you will begin to see a pattern emerge of how you see your worthiness and why.

If you are hitting the truth, you will most likely experience tears. Don't let this frighten you. This is a good thing. There is power in tears. It just means you are beginning to discover the pain those lies have caused you. Remember: there are no right or wrong answers. All that is required is being as honest as you can with yourself.

When you are done exploring, take some time in your safe space and envision your Higher Self and love surrounding you. Allow your Higher Self to mirror your lovability. You want to feel this love as deeply as you can. If new images or people show up to offer this love, just allow it.

When I was working on my lovability, I would envision my Higher Self running toward me with open arms. She would be so excited to see me that she couldn't wait to throw her arms around me. This gesture helped me immensely to begin to understand, and more importantly to begin to *feel*, how lovable I was in the universe's eyes.

Just as I did in my meditations, use your imagination to envision what lovability looks and feels like for you. Remember: your Higher Self will use your imagination to bring forward what you need to find your way back to love. So don't wait for something to happen when you are doing the loving section of the meditation; work with your imagination to create whatever images you need to feel the flavor of love you are working on connecting with in that moment.

Remember: the end goal is not to just feel your pain but also to begin to transform it with the power of love. Yes, you certainly may feel better having vented your emotions, but you want to replace that old energy with new energy of love. So don't rush this ending to your meditation. When you are done, thank yourself for taking the time to do this work, and thank your Higher Self for its help and love.

Okay, put music on if you wish, get comfy, and close your eyes and explore your feelings on your worthiness of love.

Final Thought

Remember when working with your lovability that it has absolutely nothing to do what you have done or will do. It is about your core essence. For some this will be hard for the simple reason that we often look at actions as proof of a person's worth. But when working on self-love, you will begin to understand that actions have less to do with a person's worth and more to do with his or her state of self-love or lack thereof.

You will begin to understand that the times you behaved badly had nothing to do with what was happening in the present situation and everything to do with what was happening inwardly. Almost all destructive actions can be traced back to a lack of self-love. There is no greater fear for many than the fear that others will find out they are not lovable, loving, or loved.

Every being on the planet is worthy of love. Worthiness of love is not about being good or bad. Those are ego judgments. Spiritually, your very existence affords you the birthright of being worthy of love. It doesn't matter if no one around you sees you as lovable. The universe does and longs for you to return to that truth. Be brave and begin to see yourself as the universe does—as a most lovable member of the universe's family.

Your Homework

Take notice throughout your week of where and how many times lovability or not being worthy of love is mirrored in your life either in your thoughts and actions or in others around you, as well as in what you read or watch on TV or online. Especially take note of when you mentally decide you or someone else is not deserving of being treated with love.

In your safe space, investigate how it has felt to feel unworthy of love. Use what happens throughout each day to go deeper in your exploration of what you feel and think about the fact that your existence makes you automatically worthy of love. Use your outer world as your mirror for your inner work.

Begin to discover how feeling unlovable has shaped your behavior and choices. Has it caused you to stay in relationships that weren't necessarily good for you? Explore why it is so hard to believe that the universe sees you and all others as always being worthy of love. Does this idea frighten you? Is there a part of you that is adamant that love must be earned? Do you fear what others will say or do if you decide to believe you are lovable in the universe's eyes? Take notice of all the various voices in your head that struggle with the idea that you are lovable.

Work with your Higher Self. The more you allow your Higher Self to love you, the easier it will be to shed the lie that you are not lovable. After all, you have this unconditionally loving presence that is not only willing but also delighted to love you so use it!

This will aid you in putting a stop to evaluating your worthiness of love through other people's reactions to you and instead allow you to choose to see yourself as your Higher Self sees you: as a being worthy of all the love the universe has to offer.

When you see conditions put on your, or others', worthiness of love, immediately declare, "That is a lie." Then silently say the following affirmation:

> *I am worthy of love at all times.*
> *I am lovable in both my Higher Self's*
> *and the universe's eyes.*
> *And there is nothing I can do to ever change that.*

This action will aid you in consciously observing your life and detecting what is going on around you rather than blindly going through your day. It will also set your intention on moving into worthiness versus not being worthy.

NOTES

Chapter 6

What does it mean to know you are a loving person?

To know you are a loving person is to recognize that a natural benevolence resides in your heart, always ready to be expressed uniquely through you.

Let me repeat that I am not concerned with actions or behaviors born out of a lack of self-love. You will forgive those later. I am talking about our very natures. Actions can be forgiven and changed, but our natures are constant. By nature, we are all loving beings.

Children display this benevolence when they feel compelled to rescue a bird that has fallen or bring home a stray or hurt animal. They don't worry about the logistics, as their parents may; they just know they must do something. It is their loving nature that causes them to take action.

I have seen this connection in gardeners as they are pruning their gardens. I have seen it when artists or writers are creating a new project. I have seen it in communities that come together to clean up a neighborhood. I have seen it on the streets when a homeless person shares a sandwich with another. I have seen it again and again when disasters happen around the world. We don't worry if the people we are helping look like us or think like us or even are our friends. We just feel the need to help. I have even seen it when a sappy commercial has brought a tough guy to tears. We are, by nature, loving.

So what happens that makes us doubt that we are loving people? Or, more aptly put, what makes us think our love is not good enough? Something in childhood may have made us begin to doubt ourselves and the power of our love. When parents split up, children can decide that they didn't love their parents good enough. If anger or violence is present in the home, children may wrongly decide they are responsible for it. Sometimes children are told day after day that another's pain is their fault or that they are just bad. Whatever the case, somewhere along the way many of us make the decision that our love is not good enough and that we are not as loving as other people.

I know a man that as a child was scolded terribly for sharing some of his candy with another child. The parent, who was struggling just to put food on the table, reacted from that sense of lack when he scolded the child. However, for the child, who didn't know the reason behind the reaction, he felt guilt and shame for his loving nature. While the father allowed his loving to be cut off by feelings of lack and fear, the boy expressed his loving nature by wanting to share his abundance with another. The boy was living his natural benevolence. The father was not.

You may have buried your benevolent nature just as the father did in that instance, but that does not mean it is not still there, waiting to be expressed. Even the biggest bully you have ever met has the natural tendency toward benevolence; it has simply been tucked away for safekeeping. When you have been beaten down by life or felt life has done you wrong or that you don't matter, you will not feel it is safe for you to behave lovingly. You believe you must be on guard at all times, for life is out to get you.

When you meet someone who is confrontational or defensive, just know that it is all bravado. Underneath that "tough as nails" exterior is someone who desperately longs to know that she or he is a loving person and that her or his loving is more than good enough.

I know someone who felt responsible for her mother's pain. One minute the mother, who was addicted to pills at the time, would be fine, and the next minute, she would be in a full-blown tantrum, saying the most horrible things to her daughter. She would not be not happy until she had cut her to the core. Somehow, in her mind, all her pain was her daughter's fault. No matter how hard the daughter tried to do and say the right things to keep her mother from going off, it never worked. Because this went on throughout her entire childhood, the daughter made an unconscious decision that her love hurt others. None of this was true, but to a child it was the only thing that made sense.

There are many reasons we cut ourselves off from our loving nature, but it is always there, waiting to be reclaimed. And just like lovability, the belief in your own benevolence and the idea that the expression of that benevolence is more than good enough must come from inside you. If you look for proof in the outside world, you will inevitably get mixed reviews. You cannot force someone to accept the loving you are offering. You have no idea of the baggage they carry that may be separating them from the ability to receive. But from the universe's perspective, the only perspective that matters, you are love incarnate, born with a benevolent heart, yearning to express that benevolence in all that is created and experienced.

Uncovering the truth about your inherent loving nature is paramount to self-love. You must be willing to understand the lies you were told about yourself, as well as the lies you continue to tell yourself now, and change them for the truth.

It will also be important to change your view of the world, which was born out of the idea that being loving is not part of our human nature. It may take some work to remove the barriers you have put in place, but you can rediscover your loving nature. Rest assured that your love is more than good enough to the universe!

QUESTIONS TO INVESTIGATE

1) Can you believe that you are a loving being by nature?

_____

_____

_____

_____

2) Have you ever had your heart touched by something you saw or read?

_____

_____

_____

_____

3) Can you remember a time when you were moved to act out of love with no regard for personal gain or acknowledgment?

_____

_____

_____

_____

4) Were you ever complimented when you did something out of love?

_____

_____

_____

_____

5) Were you ever shamed or scolded when you did something out of love?

_____

_____

_____

_____

6) Who first told you or made you feel that you didn't love well or correctly?

_____

_____

_____

_____

7) Were you ever blamed for another's mood or reactions? If so, why?

_____

_____

_____

_____

8) Were you ever made to feel that you were just a bad person or a black sheep?

_____

_____

_____

_____

9) Have you ever felt as though your love actually hurt others?

_____

_____

_____

_____

10) Have you ever felt the desire to help someone even though you might not know the person or even like the person?

_____

_____

_____

_____

11) Have you ever witnessed an unwarranted kind act toward another? How did seeing that make you feel?

_____

_____

_____

_____

12) Can you remember a time when your presence made someone smile?

_____

_____

_____

_____

13) Can you consider that whatever horrible things happened in your childhood had absolutely nothing to do with you? If not, why not?

_____

_____

_____

_____

14) Can you believe that everyone is loving by nature and that perhaps, like you, others too have believed lies they have told themselves about who they are and the world around them? If not, why not?

_____

_____

_____

_____

15) What do you believe is your biggest obstacle to believing you are a loving person and that your loving is good enough?

_____

_____

_____

_____

16) What would have to change in your life if you recognized your loving nature?

_____

_____

_____

_____

17) What relationship would have to change if you believed you are a loving person and your loving is good enough?

_____

_____

_____

_____

18) Do you share your loving nature with some and refuse to share with others? If so, why?

_____

_____

_____

_____

19) Does the idea of revealing your loving heart to others frighten you? If so, why? What do you fear would happen?

_____

_____

_____

_____

20) How would you move through the world differently if you allowed your loving nature to lead the way?

_____

_____

_____

_____

MEDITATION EXERCISE

Through meditation, begin to explore your feelings around your loving nature. How hard is it for you to believe that you, as well as every single person alive, have benevolence within your nature? Explore the times you were moved to lend a hand or offer a smile. Look at your parents and how they expressed or repressed their loving natures.

Can you remember a time when you were shamed or scolded for offering love to another? How did that make you feel? Were you ever blamed for not loving well enough or for not loving in the right manner? How did that change your view of the power of your love? Have you ever felt your love was somehow harmful to another? Have you ever tried your best to love someone out of his or her pain? When it didn't work (which it never does), did you decide it was your fault?

For some of you who have been severely damaged by life, it may be hard to imagine a time when you felt benevolent toward anything, because you are filled with so much rage at the world and how it has treated you. But I promise that if you go far enough back in your life, you will begin to remember a time when you were soft and gentle and when kindness was your automatic response.

Even if you recall only one time, it is enough to remind you that you acted loving once and that, underneath all your defenses, you still are a loving person. Again I stress there are no right or wrong answers. All that is required is being as honest as you can with yourself.

Call in your Higher Self and ask it to help you to discover this benevolent side of yourself. Share with it your fear of loving wrongly or not well enough. Imagine how this part of you that knows every inch of your heart would respond. Perhaps your Higher Self brings forth forgotten memories of the times your love made a difference in someone's life or how you helped a stranger. Perhaps it will simply show you the light that lives within your heart or lovingly whisper that it was not your fault and that your love is good enough. Allow your imagination to bring forward whatever your heart has longed to hear and feel.

When I was working on removing the lies about my loving nature, my Higher Self would bring forward memories of past times when my kindness, generosity, or tenderness had touched someone. I had formed some funky beliefs out of my core wounds. So when she brought these loving memories forward, they helped me to begin to understand that the expression of my loving nature was not only good enough but had also actually made a positive difference in many people's lives. If you will work with your Higher Self, I am sure he or she will remind you how your loving nature has made a positive difference as well.

When you are done, finish with love. This time call in even more elements of love. Call in images or beings that you can imagine are delighted with your presence. It may be hard, but make it up. Perhaps you might call in someone who has passed on who adored you, loving religious figures, or angels. You can also just use your Higher Self.

Let these images love you and celebrate the you that is underneath the masks you show the world. Imagine beaming faces delighted by being with you. Then see the truth in their eyes that you are a loving person whose expression of that love is more than good enough. When you are done, thank yourself for taking the time to do this work, and thank your Higher Self.

Okay, put music on if you wish, get comfy, and close your eyes and explore your feelings around your loving nature.

FINAL THOUGHT

Our ability to be loving beings is part of our spiritual DNA. While we may have locked it away in order to protect ourselves from pain or disappointment or put conditions onto it in order to follow social rules or certain religious dogma, the fact is that we all come into this world with a predisposition toward benevolence.

Opening up again to your loving nature takes the willingness to be vulnerable. Not everyone is going to respond well to your benevolence. Just as the father mentioned earlier reacted from a place of fear and lack to his little boy's benevolence, others may also have negative reactions to your benevolence. It is not your job to get anyone to receive or approve of your loving.

If your loving nature is not being received well, don't let that be your excuse for judging your loving as not good enough or, worse, cause you to shut yourself off from this part of your being. Just wish that person no harm and move on. There will be many others who will be more than happy to receive and even celebrate your benevolent nature. Your job is simply to keep connected to and to keep expressing your loving nature.

How we express our love is not important. We all are different, and therefore our loving will be different. What is important is to know that your unique expression of your loving nature is good enough and perfect to the universe—just as you are good enough and perfect to the universe.

Your Homework

Take notice throughout your week of where and how many times your ability to be loving or the wrongness of your love is mirrored in your life either in your thoughts and actions or in others around you, as well as in what you read or watch on TV or online.

Observe what happens to you when you are criticized at work or at home. Do you automatically take the criticism as an attack on your very being, subconsciously feeling attacked for not being good enough? Or are you able to separate and see the criticism as what it is—an opinion on your action but not your core nature?

Observe when you are willing to share your loving nature and when you are not. Are some people worthy of experiencing your loving nature while others are not? Also, what determines when it is safe to share your benevolence and when it is not safe to share it.

Everything going on in your life and your resulting reactions will reveal what you believe about yourself and what you desperately want to hide from others. Also notice what masks you put in place to keep people from knowing your dark secret: that you believe you are not good enough and that there is something terribly wrong with how you love.

Return to meditation to continue to explore your feelings and beliefs concerning your loving nature. Look deeper into why you believe what you believe. Examine who or what made you feel something was wrong with your loving and why you believed them then and still believe them now.

Keep working with your Higher Self to understand and redefine what it means to be a loving person. Allow your Higher Self to reveal how he or she sees your ability to love and the impact your love has on those around you, as well as the world.

When you witness someone or something doubting your loving nature, immediately declare, "That is not true." Then silently say the following affirmation:

I do have a loving heart.
I am by nature loving.
And my loving is more than good enough.

This action will aid you in consciously observing your life and detecting what is going on around you rather than blindly going through your day. It will also set your intention on moving into owning your benevolence rather than denying it.

NOTES

Chapter 7

What does it mean to know you are loved?

To know you are loved is
      to understand that your
existence has value and that
you matter to the universe.

The third and final component of self-love is the inner knowing that you are loved. This component can be a bit tricky in that we think we need another person in order to experience the feeling of being loved. However, that is not true. Self-love cannot depend on another person. Relationships change. People leave. If your feelings of being loved are contingent on who is in your life in the moment, you are setting yourself up for a life of constantly seeking validation and therefore handing over your power to another. It must come from inside of you. So how do you know you are loved?

Some people can get that sense of value from their religions. Although I have found that in some of the various religions, you have to meet certain requirements in order to be loved by whatever version of god they are worshipping. This seems a bit strange to me, in that love by its very nature is unconditional. To put certain conditions on whether you can be loved or not is incongruent to the very nature of love. Having said that, I am not saying you cannot feel loved within your particular religious choice. I would hope that you are feeling loved by your religion.

However, when talking about self-love, you must know that your value has absolutely nothing to do with what you do, what faith you practice, or how much money or power you possess and everything to do with who you are—a valued and integral part of the universe.

An atheist can just as easily experience the feeling of being loved by marveling at the complexity that came perfectly together to create his or her existence, knowing it took the perfect mix of DNA and cells and timing to give that person life. The feeling of being loved comes not from being validated from the outside but rather from the recognition that your very presence has intrinsic value. Simply put, the universe doesn't make mistakes. You were meant to be here. You are that important.

As spiritual person, I believe we incarnate in order for our souls to grow and learn, always working to bring more love and light to ourselves and our planet. You may never actually know how your presence is important to the bigger picture until you cross over, but you must understand that you are here on purpose. You are unique. There is not another person like you. You have been given all the traits and characteristics that were needed to set you on your path toward your greatest growth toward love. There is nothing random about you being alive or being who you are.

We are all valuable whether we know it or not. A person who has millions is no more valuable to the universe than the homeless person. Both have equal value. Your first response to this may be "No way. The millionaire built buildings and created jobs. The homeless person is just a bum adding nothing of value to this world. How can he possibly be valued the same as the millionaire?"

First off, you are judging something from a human egoistic perspective. You are still seeing value as something to be earned. What you can't see is the bigger picture. The universe is not interested in whether you are a prosperous or successful member of society. What the universe is interested in is *you*. Period.

The soul housed in that disheveled, crumpled body living on the street may not have the money or power of the millionaire. However, through his soul's wisdom, he willingly took on the mantle of the helpless in order to awaken compassion in all that pass him, as well as to learn whatever lessons he came specifically to learn.

In the same vein, you can't judge the millionaire for not being valuable simply because he made millions while others went without. You don't know what he or she came to learn or what impact the millionaire had on others' growth. There is always much more going on than meets the eye.

Some of you might say, "I understand the idea about the bum, but what about a murderer? No way does the universe value him. He can't matter. After all, he is a murderer!" Again I say you can't see the bigger picture. If you happen to believe in reincarnation, as I do, you will understand the idea that the murderer is just playing the other side of the victim coin to aid his soul in growth and wisdom. If you believe in the Christ energy, as demonstrated by Jesus, you know love was offered to all people including those that society deemed as unworthy.

All religions, in some form or another, define god as love and express that this love is unconditional. So if that is true, which I believe it is, then of course the murderer is loved and valued by the universe. I repeat:

there is much more going on than meets the eye. It is not important for you to know what is going on; it is just important for you to know that the universe loves every single person. The bottom line is that if you are here, you have value to the universe and are loved. And nothing you do or say will change that!

To begin to understand your value and that you matter to this planet and the universe, you will have to explore not only your beliefs around personal value but also the divine and what it means to be alive. These are deep questions but are vital to your ability to love yourself and see yourself as a valued member of the human race and beyond.

No matter what you choose to believe concerning the divine or the universe, you must begin to examine which ideas or beliefs expand your feelings of self-love and value, and which ideas and beliefs constrict and devalue you. It is always your choice what you choose to believe, but I am hoping that through your self-discovery you will expand your ideas around what value is and begin to consider that perhaps you are valued not for anything you can or will do but simply because of who you are: a piece of the divine having a human experience.

QUESTIONS TO INVESTIGATE

1) What does it mean to *feel* valuable?

_____

_____

_____

_____

2) Do you value yourself? If so, how do you express that value? If not, why not?

_____

_____

_____

_____

3) Do you look for others to validate you?

_____

_____

_____

_____

4) Do you try to prove your value by what you do, what you achieve, or even whom you know?

_____

_____

_____

_____

5) What would happen to your value if you lost everything that has come to define you?

_____

_____

_____

_____

6) Do you think you have to earn value?

_____

_____

_____

_____

7) Do you believe people with more money or power are more valuable than you, or vice versa?

_____

_____

_____

_____

8) Can you believe that every single person alive is loved and valued by the universe? If not, why not?

_____

_____

_____

_____

9) Has anyone ever told you he or she wishes that you hadn't been born, that you were a mistake, or that you were useless?

_____

_____

_____

_____

10) Did you believe that person? If so, why?

_____

_____

_____

_____

11) How did that make you feel?

_____

_____

_____

_____

12) Can you consider that while the above-mentioned person may have not wanted you in his or her life, the universe very much wanted you to be here? If not, why not?

_____

_____

_____

_____

13) Can you consider that just being alive is purpose enough, or do you need to prove your right to be alive?

_____

_____

_____

_____

14) Have you ever spontaneously felt loved for no apparent reason?

_____

_____

_____

_____

15) What is the biggest obstacle keeping you from believing that you are loved and that you matter to the universe?

_____

_____

_____

_____

16) Who told you or treated you as if you were not valuable?

17) Can you consider that this was a lie and simply a reflection of what the person believed about himself or herself? If not, why not?

18) Do you believe life is random, or do you believe it is organized?

19) Is the universe a benevolent universe or an uncaring (survival-of-the-fittest) universe?

20) Do you believe in the divine?

_____
_____
_____
_____

21) What do you believe about the divine?

_____
_____
_____
_____

22) Are there rules you must obey to be loved by the divine?

_____
_____
_____
_____

23) What happens if you don't know or follow the rules?

_____
_____
_____
_____

24) Did the divine somehow make you wrong?

_____
_____
_____
_____

25) Does the universe reward some and punish others?

_____

_____

_____

_____

26) Who taught you about the divine?

_____

_____

_____

_____

27) Have you expanded or changed your viewpoint on the divine or simply kept what was taught to you as a child?

_____

_____

_____

_____

28) What would happen if you chose to expand your definition of the divine or how the universe works?

_____

_____

_____

_____

29) Does the divine know your name?

_____

_____

_____

_____

30) Do you matter to the universe? If not, why not?

_____

_____

_____

_____

31) Does the universe care about your dreams? If not, why not?

_____

_____

_____

_____

32) Is your first response to a difficulty to beg God to rescue you?

_____

_____

_____

_____

33) What happens if that rescue doesn't arrive? How does it affect your belief that you are loved and valued by God?

_____

_____

_____

_____

34) Have you ever considered that God, knowing you have been fully equipped for your journey, wants you to wake up to your power and to use that power to rescue yourself? If not, why not?

_____

_____

_____

_____

35) If God is love and God is everything, then what does that make you?

_____

_____

_____

_____

36) If you knew the only thing stopping you from feeling loved was yourself, would you make the changes necessary to get out of your own way?

_____

_____

_____

_____

37) Who would you piss off if you chose to believe you were loved just for being you?

_____

_____

_____

_____

38) What would have to change in your life if you started to feel loved and believed you were valuable just as you?

_____

_____

_____

_____

39) How would you move through the world differently if you knew you were loved and mattered to the universe?

_____

_____

_____

_____

MEDITATION EXERCISE

Go into your safe space and invite your Higher Self to join you. Begin to explore your feelings around your personal value and your lack of feeling loved. How hard is it for you to believe you are valuable just as you are with nothing being required? Is action required to be valued? Is everyone, including people you may deem "bad," valued the same? How hard is it for you to grasp the idea that your very presence on the planet means you are valuable to the universe?

Look at your parents and their beliefs around value. Were there requirements that had to be fulfilled for you to feel valued by them? What happened when you did not fulfill those requirements? How did failing to meet expectations make you feel? Do you believe that there are expectations you must fulfill to have the universe's love? Does your religion support the idea that every human being is valued, with no exceptions? If it does not, then what does it say about you when you are not perfect?

Look for times when you may have been shamed or scolded for valuing someone when all those around you did not. It may be hard to imagine that you are valued when the people in your life have taught you that value is something to be earned or value is only for certain kinds of people. So take a look at the people in your life and honestly evaluate whether their way of being added anything to their life. Did it make them more loving and openhearted, or did it make them fearful and closed off?

Also explore whether there ever has been a time when you spontaneously felt loved for no reason. I am not talking about a time when someone made you feel loved. I am talking about a time when you were alone with yourself and had a feeling of value and love wash over you. For many this may mean going back to times in childhood when you were just playing or being creative, or out in nature. There may not be many such instances you can remember, but it takes only one for you to begin to remember that feeling.

Be willing to explore every nook and cranny of the lies you have told yourself about value and how the universe loves you. Again I stress there are no right or wrong answers. All that is required is being as honest as you can with yourself.

Finish your meditation with love, again adding even more elements and images of love. Imagine seeing yourself in the center of that love. Perhaps moonlight or stars hit you like a spotlight, bathing you in loving light and warmth. Envision being surrounded by loving beings that know you by name and beam with love for you. Make yourself the center of attention.

Perhaps your Higher Self grins from ear to ear as she or he gives you a standing ovation and cheers for you. I repeat again: make it up. It is your time to explore feeling loved and feeling that you matter, so submerge yourself in the images and feelings that make you feel the most loved, cherished, and treasured. Be the playwright of your meditation and create the scenario that is most impactful. If it touches your heart, you can rest assured that you are on the right track.

You want to create the sense that you are known, valued, and loved by the universe. Only you know, consciously or unconsciously, what images will invoke that feeling of value and love. It may take some practice, but eventually you will discover how to imagine this feeling of value and being loved for yourself. Then you can return to it whenever you need to be reminded that you are loved.

When you are done, thank yourself for taking the time to do this work, and thank your Higher Self.

Okay, put music on if you wish, get comfy and close your eyes, and explore your feelings concerning the fact you are loved for just being you.

FINAL THOUGHT

To know you are valued and loved by the universe is to feel connected to the divine that resides in all of us. And through that connection you are reminded that you matter to the universe not for what you can do or will do, but because you are an integral part of that divine energy manifesting as you.

While it may be a struggle at times to return to that feeling that you matter and are valuable, it is vital you do so to return to self-love. If you will look inward and not outward when you have doubts, you will always find your way back to the truth; you are valued by the universe simply because *you* are *you*, and you are loved beyond measure.

Understanding the universe loves and values you just as you are can empower you in so many ways. You become more forgiving of your mistakes. You release the need to be perfect because you know the universe does not demand it. How could it when your imperfections were created perfectly for your journey?

Loneliness begins to dissipate when you know the universe has witnessed your pain and tears and has been beside you through it all, always sending you love.

The need to rack up accomplishments to prove yourself to the world is replaced with accomplishments born out of joy and the self-expression of that joy.

When you truly understand that you are loved, there are no situations or people who can take that feeling of value and love away.

To accept that you matter and are valued at all times affords you the freedom to be you and to *love* being you.

I want to take a moment to mention two important things before we move on to Part 3. Firstly, because of the times we live in, I don't want anyone to misconstrue what I meant when I wrote that we all were made perfect. I was not referring to biology. I was referring to a soul and spirit level. I believe we all come in with a blueprint of what is most probably for this incarnation. It takes a brave soul to be willing to come into this life knowing he or she may well be in the wrong body and have to fight for his or her right to be who he or she feels he or she is. But I believe that fight is a noble fight—one that will open our hearts and lift up all of us. So, yes, in the truest sense, transgender people are not made wrong. They have been made perfectly for the journey their souls have chosen: to make humanity more loving and openhearted, and to mirror for all of us the beauty and courage of self-love in action. I just felt I needed to make that clear.

Secondly, I want to stress that the work that you will do doing in Part 3 is building upon the work you have done in Part 2. You will not be able to successfully move forward and do the orphan work until you have, at the very least, begun the work with the various components of self-love. It will be very hard to convince an orphaned part of yourself that he or she are lovable, loving, or loved if you have not begun to understand and feel these truths for yourself.

Your Homework

Take notice throughout your week of where and how many times your value or lack of value is mirrored in your life, either in your thoughts and actions or in others around you, as well as in what you read or watch on TV or online.

Pay attention to how you value others. This will tell you a lot about how you see value and what requirements are necessary to receive that value. What you demand of others in order to be valued and loved is what you believe the universe demands of you in order for you to be loved.

While human love is always conditional, the universe's love is not. Honestly look at what that means to your place in the universe. Perhaps you fear it makes you less special if every single person is valued and matters to the universe. And conversely, how comforting is it to know that you are known by name by the universe, and that you are valued and loved unconditionally?

Return to your safe space and continue to explore your feelings around your value. Use what comes up in your daily life as a mirror for your homework. When feelings of not being valued arise, or when you notice you are not valuing another, use those instances to go deeper into your emotions concerning your lack of value and your beliefs around what value means while in meditation.

Continue to work with your Higher Self, allowing it to teach you and show you how much you matter. Your Higher Self is your best resource for redefining love and what it feels like to be loved, so let it love you and mirror for you just how valuable you are to it and the whole of the universe.

When I was working on value, I would arrive to my safe space and my Higher Self would be standing there waiting for me. Then, as I shared my fears and tears regarding not mattering or being loved by the universe, she would smile and point up to the trees. When I looked up, I would see the branches were full of my guides and angels. There were hundreds of them! That one image did more than any words could have done to break through my walls and open my heart to my own value. I still use that image today if I need a quick reminder that I am loved.

So keep allowing your imagination to reveal what your Higher Self wants you to know. As I have said, your Higher Self will use your imagination to communicate. If your ego screams that you are making it up, just ignore it. Your ego is not your friend. Look at it this way if it helps: you have spent years making up all sorts of negative things, so why not enjoy using that same gift of imagination to make up the most positive, loving things possible? Besides, you are going to need your imagination as you begin consciously working with your emotions in part three. So keep flexing this muscle.

When you witness value being contingent on what someone does or doesn't do, immediately declare, "That is wrong." Then silently say the following affirmation:

I am valued and loved no matter what I do.
My value is never about what I accomplish.
I matter to the universe simply because I am me.

This action will aid you in consciously observing your life and detecting what is going on around you rather than blindly going through your day. It will set your intention on moving into owning your value rather than denying it. It will also free you to see others' value in a more loving, truthful way, for if you are valued for being you, so are they.

NOTES

Part 3

Investigating, Interrogating, and Integrating

Chapter 8

What do you mean by consciously working with emotions?

Consciously working with
your emotions is the process
of allowing your emotions
to guide you to your inner
wounds, and the beliefs born
out of those wounds, that are
keeping you from self-love.

You really didn't think we were done with emotions, did you? Everything we have discussed and practiced thus far was to get you to open up to what you are thinking and, more importantly, what you are feeling inside. If you have done the exercises and homework, you should be much more aware of what is going on inside of you than before you began reading this book.

Now I can hear some of you say, "Yes, I know more about my feelings, but so what? It doesn't change anything. I already knew I was angry." The reason you want to explore your feelings is so you can begin to understand what your emotions are masking

You cannot change what you refuse to acknowledge, and you can't grow beyond what you have known without understanding. For instance, if you don't understand that your anger is always masking deeper issues and beliefs, then you will just stay angry till the day you die. It is your choice, of course, but it would not be my choice of how to live.

If you don't understand that recurring patterns in your life are indicative of an inner wound needing healing, then nothing will change and you will get to experience the same energy over and over. Again, it's your choice. But I am assuming that if you are reading this, you have already made the decision that you want more out of your life and desire to be free from the pain you have been carrying around, consciously or unconsciously.

The trick to uncovering beliefs is to be brave enough to go underneath the beliefs that you are willing to share with the world. It is easy to share "I believe God loves me" or "I believe I am a good person," but underneath may be a potent belief. Yeah, God loves me, but he made me wrong" or "Yeah, I am a good person, but if anyone saw what was inside me, they would go running for the hills." We all carry old beliefs that were created out of our childhood wounds. As children, we didn't understand what was going on around us, so when something difficult or ugly happened around us or to us, we unknowingly decided what the cause was in our unformed minds. And boom! A belief was born. If the same thing happened over and over, it would end up confirming our twisted belief, which would then become part of our worldview. The more something is repeated, the firmer the belief.

One of the easiest ways to find those hidden beliefs is to look for the patterns and themes that reoccur in your life. I always attract angry people—boom: belief. I always lose out on the good jobs—boom: belief. I always have to work harder than other people—boom: belief. I can't ever have what I want—boom: belief. Underneath those beliefs will most likely be childhood issues of value, worth, as well as safety, security, and lack (issues connected with lack of self-love). We all have recurring themes in our lives (until we get the lesson), so why not be brave enough to look at the beliefs that keep drawing those same patterns back into our lives.

Another technique for finding hidden beliefs, besides checking for patterns and themes, is to pay attention to what you say to yourself. What phrases do you tend to repeat almost like a mantra when things don't go your way? Perhaps your go-to is "Life is not fair" or "I knew it; nothing good happens to me" or "I never have enough money." All of these statements are indicative of a belief that you hold concerning you and your world. The frequency and the emotional intensity with which they are repeated will determine the amount of impact they have on your reality. Paying attention to your inner dialogue will aid you tremendously in discovering the beliefs that are keeping you from experiencing a better life.

I assure you that there is nothing sweeter than being freed from a lie you have carried for way too long. Don't be surprised if you hold conflicting beliefs. That is the reason you can hear some religious people say in one breath that they believe that God is love and say in the very next breath, "Fear God." Here are two opposing beliefs in one mind—one of love and one of fear. So which one wins? Most likely it will be the one that makes us feel safer; we will only give lip service to the opposing belief.[3]

Having said all that, let's look at anger a bit closer and see where it can lead you. Let's say you are jealous of what someone else gets. You may at first feel angry and stop there, figuring, "Okay, I felt and owned that emotion. I'm pissed." But if you will follow the emotion and listen to what is running that emotion, you may begin to hear phrases such as "That's not fair," "Everyone

---

[3] McClung, J., How Learning to Say Goodbye Taught Me How to Live, 34.

else gets what they want, but never me," or "I knew there would not be enough to go around." All of these phrases indicate a core belief born out of a core wound. Feelings of unfairness, never being good enough, or lack will now be able to guide you back to where the belief began, which most likely will be a childhood wound.

When you have begun to uncover what is underneath the anger, you can then ask yourself new questions. Remember to always *feel* the answer. You will know when you have found the emotional truth to each question because you will *feel* it.

For instance, you may logically know that there is enough to go around for you, but when you begin to allow your emotions to talk to you, you may discover you fear that if you are not very careful or perfect, there will not be enough for you. In that case, you may be moving through the world articulating that there is enough for you, but your emotions are sending a signal that there is a very good chance you will lose out if you are not very careful. And guess which one ends up creating your reality—the one that has the emotional charge. Emotion always trumps lip service.

Questions to Investigate

1) Why do you feel you can't have what you want?
(Simply saying "Because it is true" or "Because it has always been that way" is not enough. Go below the surface, and list the phrases or words that pop into your mind. It will tell you a lot about what you believe.)

_____

_____

_____

_____

2) When did you decide you couldn't have what you want?
(Go as far back as you can remember being hurt by not getting what you wanted. It will most likely be a time in childhood when your heart was broken.)

_____

_____

_____

_____

3) Why do you feel it is unfair?
(Include all the reasons you believe you deserved to have it.)

_____

_____

_____

_____

4) When was the first time you felt you were not being treated fairly?
(Again look to your childhood—especially times when you felt you did your best but for whatever reason were not treated fairly through no fault of your own.)

_____

_____

_____

_____

5) Why do you feel there is never enough of certain things for you?
(Look for past instances in childhood when you were made to do without or when someone else's needs were more important than yours.)

_____

_____

_____

_____

6) When did you decide there was never going to be enough for you?

(This will be a time in your childhood when you made the decision that it would always be this way and perhaps you would possibly have to fight for everything you got.)

_____

_____

_____

_____

7) When did you decide you would have to work harder than others to get what you wanted?

(Look for the times when it appeared others seemed to receive what they wanted without working as hard as you did.)

_____

_____

_____

_____

8) How have these past instances affected you in the present?

(Look at how you handle situations that you deem as unfair or as keeping you from what you want, or where there is a sense that there is not enough to go around.)

_____

_____

_____

_____

MEDITATION EXERCISE

Go to your safe space along with your Higher Self and begin to explore one of the incidents in your childhood that triggered a strong emotional response from one of the questions in the previous section. If nothing in the questions section triggered you, then choose an incident you are aware of that hurt you in the past.

Go back to the emotionally charged time and begin to feel that emotion. As you tap into that emotion, begin to envision the part of you that is feeling that emotion. If you are not sure who is feeling the pain, ask your subconscious to bring forward the part of you in pain.

Then begin to imagine what this part looks like. Make it as real as possible. Is it a small child or an adolescent? Observe his or her appearance. Is he or she clean or dirty, strong or weak? Your emotions will reveal an appearance that usually sums up that orphan's feelings (I call this wounded part of you an orphan simply because it has been abandoned and often forgotten and lost). Don't try to see your actual self at that age. It will be a symbolic image.

Where is this orphan when you see him or her? Is the orphan out in the sunshine or alone in a cave? Again, you are not necessarily looking for the actual place the incident took place. You want your emotions to build the landscape.

Once you have the image, allow that orphaned part of you to vent his or her feelings to you on the incident with no judgment on your part. Your job is to listen. Think of it as though you are acting as his or her therapist and healer. Listen with compassion and love. Yes, you will be feeling the emotions, but you want to stay focused on what they are saying.

One of the benefits of imagining a wounded part of yourself as separate from you is that it trains you to be the observer, preventing you from getting lost in the emotion. It keeps you focused on the job at hand, which is to listen, because it is what the orphan is saying that will give the clues about why you believe and feel the way you do. By listening and observing, you will begin to understand better where your view of yourself and the world was formed and how an incident that happened when you were perhaps a six-year-old is still impacting your life.

If you do feel you are getting lost in the emotion, ask your Higher Self to help you. You can envision she or he taking your hand and pulling you back a bit from the energy. Often just the gesture of my Higher Self standing next to me was enough to keep me from getting lost in the emotion and becoming that six-year-old. I of course still felt the emotion and shed tears, but I was able to remain the investigator and not become the victim.

Offer the orphan comfort as you listen. If he or she will allow it, hold the orphan as you and he or she cry. You would be amazed how soothing a simple "I know and I am so sorry" or "I understand, and that should have never happened to you" can be. You don't want to stop him or her in these early "getting to know you" meetings, but you can let him or her know you care. It will begin to build trust between this orphan and you. It will be a lot easier to work with your inner orphans to unmask your childhood wounds when they know they won't be judged and that there is a steady, firm, and loving hand reaching out to them.

When you feel you have heard and felt what your orphan has to say (for the time being), let him or her know he or she is not alone and that you are sorry for his or her pain. Assure your orphan you have heard him or her and will return again to help him or her. Tell your orphan you love him or her, and remind your orphan that he or she is *safe* now.

I usually ended these early healing meditations by putting my orphans in lovely safe spaces surrounded by loving images of nature or angels or whatever the little ones needed to feel safe and loved.

One of my orphans, whom I had found dirty and hiding in a cave in the beginning, just wanted to have kittens and puppies all over her, so of course, that is what I gave her. As I gained her trust, she eventually greeted me out in the open with kittens in her pockets, puppies in her hands, and a smile on her face.

Don't forget to also take some time to allow your Higher Self to shower you in love. If you did the work and tapped into the pain, you will need some calming love. Allow your Higher Self to offer words of comfort and some nurturing for your pain. You will need to know your Higher Self is sorry for your pain just as you were sorry for your orphan's pain. Take the time to let your Higher Self's love into your heart. Again, make it up. You are learning to offer yourself the love your heart desires. This heart work is transformational, so don't skip it!

When you are done, thank yourself for taking the time to do this work, and thank your Higher Self.

Okay, put music on if you wish, get comfy and close your eyes, and imagine an orphaned part of yourself.

Final Thought

As you can see in the questions section, each question gets you closer to the truth and can eventually take you back to the time when you decided as a child that this is the way the world works for you. When you know the truth about why you believe something about yourself or the world, only then can you choose to change it to a more loving, empowering belief or worldview. That is why you want to get comfortable with working with your emotions—to be free to choose for yourself!

The emotional landscape and orphan work is vital not only to understanding your beliefs but also allowing your emotional body to begin to clear itself of old trapped emotions. Like a drain that has been clogged for years, your past highly charged emotions need to be expressed. By allowing them to be expressed, you are removing the power they have held over you. Denying or dismissing your inner pain will change nothing.

I want to remind you once again that when you are working with your orphans, it is very easy to end your meditations after you have allowed the repressed emotions to be expressed. There can be a feeling of lightness and freedom just from the act of expressing your feelings. However, just venting emotion is not transforming or healing the wound. Lasting changes happen only through working with love. So don't lose focus on the end goal of replacing that pain with love.

If you are willing to roll up your sleeves and feel what you have been carrying around for years, you will begin to understand yourself better. It is through this understanding of yourself and why you are the way you are that you will begin to feel compassion for yourself. As you continue to unmask and heal your old wounds, you will eventually be able to use that compassion to forgive the past, thus freeing you to return to self-love. You then will be able to create and experience your life from that truth instead of from the pain and the lies the wounds created.

YOUR HOMEWORK

Take notice throughout your week where and how many times the particular issue you worked on comes up in your daily life. Pay attention to how this issue is mirrored in your thoughts and actions or in others around you, as well as in what you read or watch on TV or online.

Return to your orphan in meditation along with your Higher Self. It is especially important to do so if you experience an intense emotional reaction in your daily life. Listen and offer comfort. Give your orphan a safe space to vent all of his or her feelings and emotions with no restraint. Allow your orphan to kick or scream or hit if that is what he or she needs to do. Although you will be feeling the emotion, remember that your job is to listen so you can discover the beliefs born out of their fear and pain.

Continue to offer your orphan love and comfort and remind him or her how sorry you are for what he or she has gone through. This will begin to build trust. Also keep getting the same love and compassion for you from your Higher Self. Allow yourself to be as vulnerable with your Higher Self as your orphan is with you.

Your whole goal is to get intimate with these parts of yourself so you can understand their viewpoints (beliefs) and bring healing to these parts of yourself in pain. Then you will be able, through the work you do with your Higher Self, to truly change the negative beliefs you have carried for so long to more positive, self-loving beliefs.

As always, end these healing meditations with love for both you and your orphan.

During your day, when you witness those feelings of pain arising to the surface, take a deep breath and silently say the following affirmation:

I will and I am healing this pain.
I understand this pain is my responsibility.
I know, right now, I am safe, secure,
and surrounded by love.

This action will aid you in consciously observing your life and detecting what is going on around you rather than blindly going through your day. It will also set your intention on the empowerment of healing yourself rather than blaming those around you and will remind you that in the present you are choosing love.

NOTES

Chapter 9

Why do I have to unmask my childhood or old wounds?

To return to self-love,
    you must be willing to
heal and transform any old
wounds that are keeping you
from the truth that you are
lovable, loving, and loved.

I understand that returning to past wounds is something most people don't want to do. They think, like the old saying, "Out of sight, out of mind." They believe that if they ignore the past, it will not have any impact on them. That simply is not true. Your past, and its impact on your ability to love yourself, formed your viewpoint not only about yourself but also about how the world works and how you believe the world will treat you. It formed your opinions about what love is, what love looks like, and, most importantly, what love *feels* like.

You can't return to self-love if you are unwilling to even look at your wounds. There is no disgrace in admitting that you have unhealed wounds from the past. We all have wounds from our childhood: some small and insignificant but others life-altering. The life-altering wounds (or core wounds) came about when we decided something was wrong with us and that the world was not safe for us.

Out of those core wounds, we construct a belief system of how to behave in order to be safe or to earn love. It is out of those core wounds that we set up our defenses and safety nets to aid us in moving through an unpredictable and possibly dangerous world. It is out of those core wounds that we lose our power and begin to look outside of ourselves for proof of our value and worth, as well as proof that our love and ourselves are good enough.

Your wounds are not something that just happened back when; they are still happening every single day through the pain you still carry deep within; through the beliefs born out of that pain; and through the choices you make because of that pain.

If you want to return to self-love, you must free yourself from the past, and that means you must heal your wounds—not ignore them. You have parts of yourself that have been orphaned and are just waiting to be rescued and reunited with you. They desperately want to be acknowledged and heard. These orphaned parts need your help in understanding what happened to them and that it wasn't their fault. They are longing to know you love them and that the universe cares.

To return to those orphaned parts of you and rescue them from the pain and lies they still are trapped in is the ultimate act of self-love. Just as anyone in his or her right mind would stop and help a wounded child, your inner orphans are crying out for you to love them enough to rescue them and offer much-needed healing and love. As you become more comfortable with your emotions, you will use those emotions to reconnect to these orphaned parts of yourself.

As I wrote earlier, your job is to investigate, interrogate, and eventually integrate all the parts of yourself in pain. You have already begun practicing investigating techniques by listening and paying attention to what is going on inside of you when emotions are triggered, and asking yourself questions— the "but whys." You, of course, will continue using these techniques when working with your orphaned parts.

However, rather than just listening and consoling, you now will begin to dialogue with them—to interrogate these orphaned parts. When they are venting emotions, you will ask them questions, much like you did with yourself in the questions sections.

For example, if your child is shouting about how unfair the world is, you will ask him or her why he or she feels that way or who told him or her that. Don't be surprised if his or her answer differs from the one you expected or has elements you have forgotten or deemed unimportant. Just as a therapist would question you to find out the root of your problem, you will do the same with your orphaned parts.

It is through this dialoguing, or interrogating, that you will begin the process of integrating these orphans back into wholeness. As you uncover the truth of what they feel and believe, you will begin to counter their "lies" with the truth that they are lovable, loving, and loved—and always have been. You will offer them an alternative viewpoint as to what happened to them and why.

For example, Let's say your father used to scream horrible things at you. Your little one, or inner orphan, may have decided that it was his or her fault because he or she wasn't lovable. You, as an adult, know your father was an alcoholic, or maybe you now know your father was full of rage as a result of how his life had turned out. You will share this information with your orphan in a manner that he or she can understand. Just as you would choose your words in accordance with the maturity of a child you are speaking with, you will chose the words most appropriate for your orphan.

Your inner five-year-old may just need to know it was not his or her fault and that he or she is very lovable to you and god. It was just something was wrong with daddy and it had absolutely nothing to do with him or her. The inner thirteen-year-old will want to understand more and may even demand to know why the universe didn't care about him or her. If you have not expanded your viewpoint on god or the universe, this questioning from your orphan will force you to do more exploring of your beliefs and feelings around the divine before you will be equipped to help your orphan. You can't help your orphan know the universe loves him or her, or that he or she matters, if you have not, at the very least, begun to understand that truth for yourself.

As you can see, this work is not linear so much as it is circular. You and your orphan are teaching one another and helping each other to discover and remove whatever is keeping you separated from love. When you hit one of those moments, consult with your Higher Self. It is your best resource for a higher, wiser viewpoint and the best source of unconditional love. Your Higher Self will teach you so you, in turn, can teach your orphan.

Remember: you are not waiting for some voice outside of yourself. Your Higher Self is the part of you that is intimate with unconditional love and all its characteristics. Just as you are playing the part of the orphan, you are also playing the part of your Higher Self. So use your imagination to aid you in discovering what a being rooted in unconditional love would say on the subject. You will know when you have found the truth because it will crack open your heart and tears will flow.

I know it can sound complicated. However, the process is simply one of getting to know these parts and offering them love and a new viewpoint on love. Think of them as if they are foster children, arrived at your doorstep, whom you must get to know. Then, once you have their trust, you have to get them to believe they are lovable, loving, and loved. Believe it or not, you will find a way to do that because you love these children and want only the best for them.

If a foster child were to ask you something you didn't have the answer to, as children always do, you would do your research with your Higher Self before giving it an incomplete or insincere answer. It is the same thing with your orphans. If you don't have the answer, you know you have some work to do on your own before you can help them.

As you begin to fall in love with your orphaned parts (and you will!), you will find your way. Just trust that you will know how to talk to these parts, even if it means you have to go back and do some work on yourself first. You will be amazed at the wisdom and the depth of love that arises from within you as you are working with your inner orphans.

I know this can sound daunting, and it is going to take some patience on your part. This healing work will not happen in just one meditation session. It is a process. It will take time and diligence. But how much more daunting is it to live the rest of your life in pain and disempowerment?

By acknowledging the orphans' pain through your shared tears, comforting them with compassion as only you can, and offering them new viewpoints based on self-love, you will be healing these wounded parts of yourself once and for all. Not only will you be freeing them to live the truth, but you will be freeing yourself as well.

If you are still carrying pain from your childhood or adolescent years, it is time to lift up the veil and bring those lost parts into the light and allow them to shine again. The following questions will aid you in discovering those wounded and orphaned parts and give you a jumping-off point for your healing meditative work. The good news is that if you did the last exercise, you have already begun to discover one or more of those orphaned parts for yourself.

QUESTIONS TO INVESTIGATE

1) Are you aware that you are carrying any pain from the past?

_____

_____

_____

_____

2) When that pain gets triggered by outside forces, what do you usually do with the pain?

_____

_____

_____

_____

3) Have you ever blamed another person for triggering your hidden pain?

_____

_____

_____

_____

4) Have you ever told someone not to "go there"? If he or she did anyway, what was your reaction?

_____

_____

_____

_____

5) As a child, did you ever feel abandoned, shamed, treated unfairly, violated, controlled, or bullied?

_____

_____

_____

_____

6) As a child, how did you explain these actions to yourself?

_____

_____

_____

_____

7) How did this change your view of yourself?

_____

_____

_____

_____

8) How did this change your view of the world and of other people?

_____

_____

_____

_____

9) Have you ever questioned the beliefs that you have built your world upon? If not, why not?

_____

_____

_____

_____

10) What do you fear might happen if you question your beliefs?

_____

_____

_____

_____

11) Are your beliefs built around safety, earning love, or proving your worth or value?

_____

_____

_____

_____

12) When a childhood wound has been triggered by something in your present, have you ever allowed yourself to observe what the awakened part of you is shouting? If not, why not?

_____

_____

_____

_____

13) What do you think would happen if you paid it some attention?

_____

_____

_____

_____

14) Can you believe you can dialogue with a younger part of yourself in pain?

_____

_____

_____

_____

15) Can you believe that an orphaned part of you is waiting for you to help it out of its pain? If not, why not?

_____

_____

_____

_____

16) Can you have compassion for those lost and hurt parts, or do you see them as weak or unimportant?

_____

_____

_____

_____

17) If you knew you could be free from the past and all its ramifications by owning and healing those hurt and orphaned parts of you, would it cause you to quit ignoring them? If not, why not?

_____

_____

_____

_____

18) Do you think the past should just be dead and buried? What would happen if you brought it out of the shadows and into the light?

_____

_____

_____

_____

19) Can you consider that the past may hold your greatest growth toward love and wisdom? If not, why not?

_____

_____

_____

_____

20) If you knew those orphaned parts stuck in pain were also the parts of you that held your passions, dreams, and love of self and the world, would you be willing to meet them and heal them?

_____

_____

_____

_____

21) What if you knew that a belief that an orphaned part of you is still holding onto is as potent, if not more so, as the belief you openly share to the world? How would that change your view of those unacknowledged parts of yourself?

_____

_____

_____

_____

22) Have you ever been told to just let go of the past?

_____

_____

_____

_____

23) How did that work out for you? Were you truly able to let it go, or did you just put it out of your mind until the next time it was brought to the surface?

_____

_____

_____

_____

24) Did putting it out of your mind actually change how you felt deep inside?

_____

_____

_____

_____

25) Can you consider that there is something to be learned from those hurt parts of you?

_____

_____

_____

_____

26) How would your life change if, instead of trying to ignore your past, you discovered you had the power to transform and integrate your past back into the wholeness that is you?

_____

_____

_____

_____

MEDITATION EXERCISE

Go into your safe space along with your Higher Self, and begin to explore one of the orphaned parts you observed in the previous exercise or one that you may already be familiar with. Again choose an emotionally charged incident to bring him or her forth. Your emotions will always be your way to connect to your inner emotional world.

Once you feel connected, again allow your orphan to start to vent his or her pain, anger, or fear with no judgment on your part; and, of course, offer them comfort. However, let's assume you have built some trust with this particular orphan over time, so you can now move out of the venting stage into interrogating and dialoguing with this part of yourself.

Just as you asked yourself questions, you are going to do the same with this orphan. By now you should be much more adept at knowing how to use questions to get to the truth. Ask the orphan why he or she feels and believes what he or she has just vented. Who told this orphan that? Why does he or she think it happened? Just as you have pushed yourself to get to the bottom

196

line, you are now going to gently push the orphan to get to his or her bottom line.

You may have heard in this orphan's venting "Nobody cared about me." But through questioning him or her, you get to the bottom line that he or she believes nobody cares about him or her because something is wrong with him or her (he or she was made wrong). With this information, you now can begin to work with this orphan to let him or her know not only that you care about him or her and love him or her just as he or she is but also that he or she was made perfectly and is valued beyond measure by the universe. If you have not begun to work on your own sense of value and being loved by the universe, you should be able to at least convey your love and value for this orphan at this time.

When I was doing interrogating work with one of my orphans, I thought I had a pretty good grasp on what the issues were and what probably would come up during our talks. However, I was surprised to find out that underneath the pain I was aware of, there was was a lie that my orphan had been secretly carrying: that god not only didn't care about her but also had forgotten she even existed. This was a bit shocking for me. I had no idea that a part of me felt that way until that moment. Needless to say, I immediately began to explore why she believed that. I also worked with my Higher Self to expand my viewpoint on god and the universe so I could offer her a more loving viewpoint. While it was not fun to discover that particular lie, I am grateful I did. It enabled me to grow my sense of value and helped me to understand just how much I do matter.

The point of this exercise is to begin to actively interact with this orphan and offer a counter viewpoint through love. Dialoguing is done not only through words but through actions as well. If your orphan feels no one cares about him or her, show this orphan he or she is wrong by hugging him or her and celebrating his or her presence. Just as you allowed your Higher Self to shower you in love in the earlier chapters, you should do the same with your orphans. Whatever you need to do to show them that they are loved and what that kind of love looks and feels like, do it.

End the session by thanking your orphan for allowing you to love him or her. Remind your orphan again that he or she is safe now and that whatever was happening to make him or her feel uncared for is over. Your orphan has you now to show him or her the truth and to love him or her. Surround this orphan in love and images that feel loving to him or her. You can also invite your Higher Self to offer him or her love if the orphan is open to it. You will know you have the right image when you see your orphan relax or go to sleep.

Then take a moment and bathe yourself in love as well. Let your Higher Self offer love to you in the manner that feels the most loving and most safe to you. Opening up to your orphans can make you feel very vulnerable. If you need to cry in your Higher Self's arms, do so. Remember: you most likely will need the same love and attention you have just offered your orphan. Perhaps you too need to hear that your Higher Self values and loves you. So don't rush this loving part. It is where the transformation is happening. I repeat: this loving is where the transformation is happening. All the other work is to make space for love.

Once you have been filled up with love, thank yourself not only for taking the time to do the work but also for having the courage to uncover and feel your wounds. Thank your Higher Self for her or his love.

Okay, put music on if you wish, get comfy and close your eyes, and meet your orphans and start a dialogue.

FINAL THOUGHT

Remember: this is a process. It may take one or ten meditations just to get one of your inner orphans to open up to you. It may take many sessions, however, for the orphan to vent enough pent-up emotions to be open enough to hear what you have to say concerning his or her situation. And it may take many sessions, before your orphan believes he or she is lovable, loving, and loved. But just as any loving parent would, keep working with them. Eventually your love and understanding will succeed in freeing your orphan from his or her pain and return him or her to feeling loved and safe because he or she has you and a loving universe on his or her side.

Also know that every orphaned part of you will behave differently. Some may be receptive to you, while others may want nothing to do with you. Just as every child in a family is unique and handles pain differently, all those lost parts of you also react to pain with their own flavor.

We are meant to be whole, and that means healing and integrating those orphaned parts of ourselves. Believe it or not, every wound holds a forgotten gem just waiting to be rediscovered. Wounds are not only filled with unhealed pain but also shroud your ability to dream and create, to feel joy and excitement, to have faith and trust, to live with passion and compassion, and, most importantly, to love and to receive love.

To live the best version of you is not to ignore certain parts of yourself. To live the best version of you is to reclaim and heal those orphaned parts and, in so doing, discover your true beauty and the ultimate power of self-love: the freedom to be you with no masks or safety nets required—just glorious you.

YOUR HOMEWORK

Take notice throughout your week as to where and how many times the orphaned part you worked with is activated or triggered in your daily life. As you become more acquainted with these orphans, you will become very aware when they get emotionally triggered. Don't let it frighten you; be grateful. It just means you are waking up.

Since you have decided to heal these parts, don't be surprised if the universe brings you situations in your life that highlight the issues you are working on with your inner orphans. Again, don't let it discourage you. Look at it as being helped to find whatever needs love and healing, which means you are not alone in this work. You have the universe and your Higher Self not only watching your back but also pointing the way.

Continue dialoguing with and interrogating your orphan in meditation, always with the intention of moving him or her toward feeling and understanding love. If you experience a wound being triggered in your daily life, allow your orphan to vent for a few minutes about what happened during the day, but then begin to dialogue with that orphan. You want to get him or her, or you, to the core of the issue rather than just staying in an emotional loop about the day's events. It can be very easy to get into a loop by staying in the venting phase of a meditation. So rather than wasting too much time on how your boss behaved, for example, get to the truth that the boss's behavior reminded you of your mother's behavior. Then you can work with the inner orphan on untangling from the past by showing your orphan how much you love him or her and how valuable he or she is to you. Remember: the goal is not to just feel and listen but also to eventually heal and integrate your orphans with love and understanding. Of course, end all meditations with receiving love for yourself as well.

During your day, when you witness those feelings of pain arising to the surface as the result of an outside trigger, take a deep breath and silently say the following affirmation:

I don't need to respond to this outside trigger.
It is simply a clue from my Higher Self. Thank you.
I know you are surrounding both me and my
orphan in love and that we are safe.

This action will aid you in consciously observing your life and detecting what is going on around you rather than blindly going through your day. It will set your intention on observing the clues all around you and on choosing healing over denial.

It will likewise help you to detect when you allow you orphaned parts and the negative beliefs they carry to impact your behavior, thereby helping you to bring your behavior out of the shadows and into the light.

NOTES

Chapter 10

Why do I have to bring my behavior out of the shadows and into the light?

In order to integrate your orphaned parts back into the whole and take your power back, you will need to own how your pain, and the beliefs born out of that pain, affected your behavior.

This work is sometimes referred to as shadow work. Bringing your shadow to the surface is the process of owning the emotions, beliefs, and behaviors you have refused to acknowledge and often unwittingly projected onto other people.

What does it mean to project your shadow onto others? Your displaced emotion will often show up in your strong reaction to other people who are expressing that emotion. If you have unexpressed anger, you will have a strong reaction to someone who is voicing anger. If you have hidden pockets of hopelessness or sadness, you will feel repelled by those emotions in other people. I think of it as the universe's way of offering a mirror through other people for us to look into and see ourselves.

Of course, no one likes being around anger, but if you have an unusually strong reaction, such as fear or condemnation, you will want to look at your unexpressed anger. If you are extremely judgmental of someone feeling sad, again you will want to look at your own hidden sadness. When we are in balance and centered in our self-love, other people's emotions have much less impact on us, and therefore our reaction is much more mild.

The good news is that you have already begun to own your emotional shadow by working with your emotions and orphaned parts in the previous chapters. That is one of the reasons it was important in the beginning of this book for you to discover what you *feel* about various emotions and begin the process of allowing yourself to express emotions that were uncomfortable or unacceptable to you. It was intended to get you to be at ease with going below the surface emotions that you were willing to own, and to begin to discover those shadow emotions.

In chapter 8, you started to uncover shadow beliefs that were masked by your emotions. You went below the beliefs you were at ease with acknowledging and began to reveal the shadow beliefs—very often the most potent beliefs one holds—you had created out of your wounds.

The next step was to get you to meet the orphaned parts of yourself and then allow them to express their pain and emotions. By their very nature, these orphaned parts live in the shadows. You may have known that parts of you were angry, but perhaps you discovered through interrogating and dialoging with these orphans that the shadow emotion underneath the anger was hopelessness born out of the shadow belief that they are not lovable and never will be. By the powerful act of listening with compassion and offering them unconditional love, you have begun to bring them out of the shadows and into the light.

As you can see, you have already begun a majority of the shadow work. The final step is now to expose how these emotions and beliefs based on self-loathing have affected your behavior. No, it may not be fun. No one likes to replay his or her "bad" behavior, but it is vital in your growth toward self-awareness and return to self-love.

As I said at the beginning of chapter 5 when I was discussing our loving nature, "Actions can be forgiven and changed, but our natures are constant." Well, the time has finally arrived to face our actions. In order to forgive and change your behaviors, you first must acknowledge the behaviors born out of your lack of self-love. I am sure that when you read you were going to have to feel your wounds, you weren't sure you could do it. But you did, or at the very least you began. By now you should know you are stronger and more courageous than you give yourself credit for.

As you work with the questions, be honest. You are looking for the times your pain caused you to behave in ways that were harmful to you or others. So be brutally honest. The only person judging you is you—more about that later.

QUESTIONS TO INVESTIGATE

1) Have you ever gone back and examined your behavior? If not, why not?

_____

_____

_____

_____

2) Does the idea of bringing your behavior out of the shadows and into the light frighten you?

_____

_____

_____

_____

3) What do you fear will happen if you own your "bad" behavior?

_____

_____

_____

_____

4) How has the feeling of being unlovable caused you to treat others?

(Look for times that as an adult something in your life caused you to feel unworthy of love or kindness, and remember how you responded to those persons or those situations.)

_____

_____

_____

_____

5) How has feeling that either you or your loving isn't good enough impacted your behavior?

(Look for the situations that triggered your feelings of being inept or wrong and how they caused you to act out against people.)

_____

_____

_____

_____

6) How has feeling unloved impacted your behavior?

(Look from the present at how you handled a situation when you were feeling unloved, unsupported, and alone. In what way did it cause you to lash out?)

_____

_____

_____

_____

7) Do you get defensive easily? What are the feelings that move you into becoming defensive?

_____

_____

_____

_____

8) Are you overly critical of others? What *feelings* trigger your criticism?

_____

_____

_____

_____

9) If you were bullied as a child, can you admit that you may become the bully at times?

_____

_____

_____

_____

10) When were the times that you too have bullied?

_____

_____

_____

_____

11) How does your bullying manifest itself?
(Do you go on the attack, become passive-aggressive, or emotionally retreat?)

_____

_____

_____

_____

12) What was going on with your orphans inside that triggered you to be a bully?

_____

_____

_____

_____

13) What was your payoff for being a bully? Did it make you feel powerful or more in control?

_____

_____

_____

_____

14) Do you wear a tough attitude or a "don't mess with me" veneer? If so, why?

_____

_____

_____

_____

15) If you knew you didn't need to behave in self-
destructive ways in order to feel safe and loved, would
you be able to change your behavior? If not, why not?

_____

_____

_____

_____

16) Do you want to be able to move through the world
with an open heart and open mind, or does that idea
scare you? If it scares you, why does it scare you?

_____

_____

_____

_____

17) What do you think you would have to give up in
order to move through the world with an open heart
and open mind?

_____

_____

_____

_____

18) Can you remember a time when you weren't defensive
or armored against the world? What did it feel like?

_____

_____

_____

_____

19) Do you believe that all behavior, including yours, can be forgiven? If not, why not?

_____

_____

_____

_____

20) If you knew self-love would allow you to forgive and let go of your defenses, masks, and safety nets, would that be okay with you?

_____

_____

_____

_____

MEDITATION EXERCISE

Go into your safe space along with your Higher Self and bring forward a memory of a highly charged time in your life that caused you to behave "badly" and treat someone "badly." Imagine and feel it as fully as you can. Remember the person and the situation that triggered you, causing you to act out.

Once you begin to feel the emotions of the situation, I want you to observe how you behaved toward that person. What words did you use to attack or punish them? What was the expression on your face—disgust, hatred, disdain? What feeling were you trying to invoke in the other person?

Perhaps you wanted that person to feel shame or guilt or sense that something was wrong with him or her, or maybe you wanted to instill fear into him or her. Gather as much detail as you can. Be brutally honest with yourself. If you wanted to cause him or her pain or harm, this is the place to admit it.

Then I want you to see the other person's face. If he or she did a good job of masking his or her emotions, imagine looking into the person's eyes. I want you to see the impact of your actions. Did you frighten that person or make him or her feel powerless or less than you? Did you hurt the person or break his or her heart? It can be painful to own your negative impact, but it is important, so stay with it.

When you have fully owned how your actions impacted this person, I want you to put your focus back onto yourself. Just as you did with the orphan work, see what was fueling your reaction to begin with. Maybe you initially felt angry over feeling attacked or criticized; perhaps you even felt your response was justified. However, when you look below the surface, what really got triggered was your feeling of not being good enough or lovable or loved. Perhaps the other person used words similar to the ones your parents used to use when talking to you. Or maybe you thought you saw a familiar look of disapproval from your childhood in that person's eyes.

You want to get to the place of being able to honestly admit to yourself that your reaction had very little to do with the other person and everything to do with you and your wounds. You will know when you are there because you will feel a sense of remorse and regret and most likely will cry. Let those feelings flow through you freely. You can even envision yourself telling the person, "I am so sorry. You didn't deserve that. I was in pain and fear."

Once you are done apologizing to the other person, I want you to take a few deep breaths and then bring the orphaned part who has been carrying the wound that got triggered in this particular instance into your space with you.

Tell your orphan you love him or her and understand why he or she got triggered. If anyone can understand why he or she reacted in such a way, it is you. Bring forward your compassion for this orphan and all the pain he or she has been carrying and the lies he or she has believed because of that pain. Let the orphan know you forgive him or her and that it is all right. You understand, and most importantly, you love him or her. You can work with him or her now, or later in a separate meditation, to further heal the issue at hand by replacing it with love and the truth of that love.

End your time by telling this orphan that he or she is safe and will always be safe from now on. Let the orphan know that he or she no longer needs to be in charge, because now that orphan has you, you will handle everything from this point forward. Then surround him or her in love and healing images.

Back in the beginning, when I would be finishing up this behavior meditation with my orphan, she was a bit doubtful that she could give up being in charge. After all, she had been on her own for so long that it was hard for her to let go of control. So when I felt her doubt that I was going to take over now, I assured her I had help by showing her my Higher Self standing beside me. Seeing this powerful and loving image beside me gave her enough confidence to let go. I rewarded her courage by ending the meditation by sending her off to theatre camp to play.

When you are done with your orphan, spend some time with your Higher Self, allowing she or he to love you. Feel its compassion for you, just as you felt compassion for your orphan. Let yourself receive forgiveness for being asleep and doing things you would not have done if you had known better at the time. Let you Higher Self remind you of your true beauty and loving nature by sharing with you how it sees you and how it has always seen you—as a being worthy of love, more than good enough in your loving and valued beyond human measurement.

End your meditation by thanking yourself for the work you have just done and for the willingness to love yourself enough to forgive yourself.

Okay, put music on if you wish, get comfy and close your eyes, and bring your past behavior out of the shadows.

FINAL THOUGHT

When you bring your past behavior out of the shadows, you have the opportunity not only to understand what makes you tick but also to begin to recognize your go-to behaviors that act as safety nets buffering you from both the outer world and your inner world of pain.

You begin to comprehend, by dissecting your own actions, how ignoring your wounds and orphaned parts has not made your life better or kept you safe. In fact, it has often made you into someone you don't even recognize or want to claim.

Once you are able to see the correlation between your inner emotions and beliefs and the "bad" behaviors they produce, you are afforded the opportunity to take yourself off autopilot and go inward, where the healing and transformation happen.

By examining your behavior, you begin to understand through compassion that you were not a "bad" person but just someone in pain who was responding to the world around him or her from that pain viewpoint.

Besides owning your impact on others, you can also use this behavior work for regrets you may still be carrying from choices you made in the past. Just as you did when working on your behavior toward others, you are going to bring forward the feelings and beliefs that were running your life at the time you made the particular regretful choice.

You will discover that the amount of hidden self-loathing and fear you were carrying at the time dictated those self-destructive choices. Just as you have felt compassion for your orphans, you will feel compassion for your twenty-year-old or forty-year-old self who also was moving through the world in pain. You will understand that from his or her viewpoint and lack of self-love, he or she couldn't have done anything differently. Fear and Pain were running the ship.

With this knowledge and compassion, you then will be able to forgive yourself and eventually offer that same forgiveness to others. For when you understand why you behaved as you did, you grow in your ability to have compassion not only for yourself but also for others who similarly are moving through the world in pain and on autopilot.

Your Homework

Take notice throughout your week of where and how many times you are on autopilot when responding to conflict or challenges. You may not be able to catch it in the moment (though you will eventually), but look back over the day at your behavior. Were there times when you didn't need to respond but you did? Honestly evaluate when you overreacted or projected your own pain and fears onto the situation. What was triggered within that caused you to respond? Look for what wound or orphan was triggered.

When something in your daily life causes you to behave badly, go into meditation and examine that behavior when you get home. As always, get to the core of the issue. Bring in the orphan that felt threatened, and dialogue with him or her. Work to discover what pain was awakened. If it was a belief that you are not good enough, remind the orphan and yourself that that is a lie.

Use whatever words you need to *feel* the truth of whatever component of self-love you are working on locking in your heart. Offer compassion, not judgment, and remind your orphan and yourself that while the behavior might have been bad, you are not.

You are simply in the process of waking up and healing. You can't expect a one-year-old to walk perfectly, so don't expect to be perfect. Remember: you are learning, so be as kind with yourself as you would with a one-year-old.

Bring in your Higher Self to offer love and understanding regarding the situation. Imagine what a being of unconditional love that knows your pain intimately and feels nothing but compassion for it, and you, would have to say. It doesn't matter if you feel you are making it up. You are teaching yourself to look inward, not outward, for all of your needs. As I indicated in the chapter on being loved, "you are so loved that the universe fully equipped you for the journey." If you need compassion or forgiveness, you *will* find it within yourself.

During your day, when you witness yourself overreacting or acting out, take a deep breath and silently say the following affirmation:

> *I forgive myself.*
> *I am simply learning to wake up.*
> *I know I reacted from the past and its pain.*
> *But right now I am in the present,*
> *and no harm can come to me.*

This action will aid you in consciously observing your life and detecting what is going on around you rather than blindly going through your day. It will set your intention on forgiving and changing your behavior. It will also remind you that you are not still in the past, experiencing the pain, but in the present with people who had no part in your wounding.

Most importantly, go to whomever you need to and apologize as quickly as possible for the overreaction. You don't have to tell those you apologize to why you overreacted; just state that you are sorry. This will create a pattern of taking responsibility and prevent you from going back on autopilot.

NOTES

Chapter 11

What are safety nets, and why can't I keep them?

Safety nets are your go-to behaviors. Safety nets are born out of the falsehood that you must protect yourself at all costs from a dangerous and unpredictable world because you are unlovable, unloving, and unloved.

Safety nets are simply formed behaviors that your ego put into place to keep you safe from the supposedly dangerous world. They are your go-to behaviors when you are feeling powerless or unloved or unlovable. These behaviors are repeated so often that the person engaging in them may not even be aware he or she is doing so. I have even heard people say, "That's just who I am," when one of their safety nets is challenged. In truth, it is not who they are at all. It is simply so routine to behave that way that they can't remember a time they didn't.

Safety nets give you a false sense of security. Unfortunately, they also keep you distanced from your true power of self-love. Each person has his or her own flavor, but many safety nets are universal and can be found running many people's lives with no understanding of why they allow it to be so. Safety nets can include the energies of control, judgment, self-righteousness, "know-it-all" or "needing to be right" conduct, a "be nice at all costs" demeanor, self-importance or self-deprecation, denial, and even anger. I include anger here because it can be used to protect you from feelings of hurt, unworthiness, powerlessness, or fear of the unknown. It is a masking emotion.

In any case, safety nets may have helped you as a child deal with what was going on around you at the time, but they will eventually cause you harm and keep you from creating your experiences from a place of self-love. They also will keep you separated from other people in some form or fashion.

231

To move into your authentic power of self-love, you have to be willing to deconstruct these safety nets by discovering what fear or belief they are masking. They are a big clue to the wounds you are still carrying and still allowing to create your reality.

So let's look at three safety nets and see what might be lying underneath them. I will not go over all of them, but this should get you started on investigating your own safety nets.

There will be questions to work with for each safety net, but there will be only one meditation exercise at the end of this chapter. You will be able to use the meditation exercise for any and all safety nets you want to bring out into the light.

SAFETY NET OF JUDGMENT

****

Judgment is nothing more than the ego's attempt to separate us from one another, thus allowing the lie that some are more valuable than others to continue permeating our world.

****

Judgment is nothing new. We have whole shows devoted to the idea of judging others, whether it is for their dress, their look, their behavior, their talent, and more. We have whole religious groups that judge those that are not part of their congregation. Judging has become a favorite pastime. We don't even question the judging; we accept it as part of our right. However, judging does nothing for our growth or our souls and can be quite detrimental to both the giver and the receiver. So why do we do it? Judging does one of two things. It either inflates or deflates the object of our judgment. We judge to feel better about something or worse about something.

When feelings of not being good enough or valuable enough rise to the surface, some people temporarily get relief from their inner loathing by taking down others. Focusing on others' "deficiencies" takes their minds off their own feelings of inadequacy and fears that they don't matter to the universe. When the judgment is turned inward, it not only acts as a barrier against change (ego loves the status quo) but also acts as a preemptive strike. You presume you will hear it from the outside world, so isn't it better coming from you? It is supposedly less painful if you admit your failings to yourself.

Underneath all judgment lies fear; fear of not being valuable and fear of not being good enough are the most common triggers. We use this safety net to either make us feel better about ourselves by putting down others or to make us feel worse about ourselves by comparing ourselves to others. In either case, it is toxic.

Judging is the ego's pastime and does nothing but separate us from others and the truth about ourselves. I also know that those that appear to be the most vocal in their judgments of others suffer the most from self-judgment. All judgment is based on the lie that somehow we are deficient or wrong in our very being.

As with all safety nets, judgment masks self-loathing and calls attention to a need to heal past wounds and negative beliefs and return to self-love.

QUESTIONS TO INVESTIGATE

1) Why do you judge other people?

_____
_____
_____
_____

2) Do you even know when you are doing it?

_____
_____
_____
_____

3) What is your temporary payoff when judging?

_____
_____
_____
_____

4) Does judging give you a sense of power?

_____

_____

_____

_____

5) Does it make you feel superior to or less than others?

_____

_____

_____

_____

6) Does it make you feel like part of a group?

_____

_____

_____

_____

7) What sense of safety does judgment give you?

_____

_____

_____

_____

8) What typically triggers you to judge yourself or
   others?

_____

_____

_____

_____

9) Does feeling different cause you to judge?

_____

_____

_____

_____

10) Do others' differences cause you to judge?

_____

_____

_____

_____

11) When not feeling good enough, do you move right into judging?

_____

_____

_____

_____

12) What happens when you lose? Do you judge the winner?

_____

_____

_____

_____

13) What happens when you win? Do you fear others will judge you?

_____

_____

_____

_____

14) What fear or supposed inadequacies cause you to turn into a judge?

_____

_____

_____

_____

15) Where did you learn to judge yourself or others?

_____

_____

_____

_____

16) How did your parents or family members handle judgment?

_____

_____

_____

_____

17) Were you praised in some form when you judged other people or groups as wrong?

_____

_____

_____

_____

18) Was judgment expected and accepted in your youth?

_____

_____

_____

_____

19) Were your parents and other authority figures constantly judging you?

_____

_____

_____

_____

20) How did being judged make you feel?

_____

_____

_____

_____

21) Have you ever considered how your judgment affects those around you?

_____

_____

_____

_____

22) How would your life be different if you let go of judgment?

_____

_____

_____

_____

Final Thought on Judgment

Judging yourself or others is a safety net; if you look underneath it, you will discover beliefs about your worth and value and more. Those who are lovingly confident in themselves have no reason or desire to judge others. They don't need to make someone less in order to feel better about themselves; nor do they feel the need to compare themselves to others.

So rather than wasting time on the surface judgment, do the homework and identify the belief you are carrying around that causes you to lose yourself in judgment. Ask yourself, "What wound does my judgment mask? What payoff do I get from judging others or myself?"

There are no winners where judgment lives, but you can learn a lot about yourself if you will uncover what is underneath your judgments.

Safety Net of Control

*Control is the ego's way of hiding
not being good enough and
feeling powerless.*

Control is never about caring too much; it is always about the fear of not being good enough and feeling powerless. Controlling others or situations is often born out of the false premise that if we don't control, we can't have what we want. Again, it is based on the lie that we are on our own in this dangerous world with no help or backup, so if we don't watch our backs, no one will, and we will be left with nothing.

So we control in order to once again feel that false sense of safety, to get our piece of the pie before none is left, and to keep anyone, especially ourselves, from knowing that we believe we are not good enough. Control can be a hard one to give up, because of its payoffs, but it is not impossible. Once you believe that you are more than good enough to the universe and that you are perfect in your imperfections, you can begin to loosen the reins on your control.

When you finally lock in the truth that you have been given everything you need for your journey, you will no longer believe you are on your own, because you will know you have a Higher Self who is watching your back! And you will finally understand you didn't need to worry about getting your piece of pie, because there is always more than enough pie for everyone.

I would like to mention that when you are in an especially difficult situation, such as a health scare or the potential loss of a career or relationship, control could be very damaging. Your ego will ramp up its need to control, although what you need to do is surrender. I know that can sound scary, but surrender is the wise choice.

> I think people misunderstand surrender. It is not saying, "Well, hell, I'm sick. I'll just surrender to the cancer and do nothing" or "I'm flat broke, so why bother dreaming and going for a more abundant life." It is quite the opposite. It is closer to saying, "I have found myself in a situation that I can't 'think' my way out of, and I have no clue, from my ego's perspective, what to do. So I surrender and call on those higher parts of my self to guide me, as they always do." You are surrendering your small, narrow viewpoint to your larger Self's viewpoint. And believe me, when you are experiencing troubling times in your life, it is your Higher Self that you want in charge, not your small frightened ego. It is the Higher Self that shows you

the beauty, love, and grace hidden in those dark times. The bottom line is that you must let go of control and surrender yourself to your Higher Self during those dark times. Your Higher Self always knows what the most loving, expanding, freeing, and comforting road is for your soul.[4]

---

[4] McClung, J., How Learning to Say Goodbye Taught Me How to Live, 20.

QUESTIONS TO INVESTIGATE

1) Why do you typically control people or situations?

_____

_____

_____

_____

2) Do you control at times because only you can do it right?

_____

_____

_____

_____

3) Do you control at times because you are afraid of others?

_____

_____

_____

_____

4) Does controlling make you feel important?

_____

_____

_____

_____

5) Does controlling give you a sense of being superior to another?

_____

_____

_____

_____

6) Do you control because if you don't, someone else will?

_____

_____

_____

_____

7) What would happen if you didn't try to control situations or others?

_____

_____

_____

_____

8) Do you believe that if you lose control, you will be hurt?

_____

_____

_____

_____

9) If you are not always in control, what will be at risk?

_____

_____

_____

_____

10) Do you tell yourself that staying in control keeps others safe even if they don't know it or like it?

_____

_____

_____

_____

11) How would your world fall apart if you weren't in control?

_____

_____

_____

_____

12) What inner emotion has triggered your need to control in the past?

_____

_____

_____

_____

13) What fear typically causes you to move into control?

_____

_____

_____

_____

14) Have you ever noticed how feeling powerless in a situation causes you to try to control the situation?

_____

_____

_____

_____

15) Do you move into control when you feel someone might be smarter or better at something than you?

_____

_____

_____

_____

16) Who or what caused you as a child to feel the need to control?

_____

_____

_____

_____

17) Have you ever sucked the life out of a relationship or situation by trying to control it?

_____

_____

_____

_____

18) How do you see surrender?

_____

_____

_____

_____

19) Is surrender giving up? If so, why?

_____

_____

_____

_____

20) Is surrender a sign of weakness or failure? Why?

_____

_____

_____

_____

21) Is surrender only a last-ditch option when you have tried everything else?

_____

_____

_____

_____

22) Is surrender only for losers and weak people?

_____

_____

_____

_____

23) Have you ever surrendered?

_____

_____

_____

_____

24) Can you remember any time when you let go of control and it turned out all right?

_____

_____

_____

_____

25) How would your life be different if you didn't need to control everything and everyone and trusted in yourself and your Higher Self instead?

_____

_____

_____

_____

Final Thought on Control

Control is born out of a victim's mentality. Once you have reclaimed your self-love, you will no longer need to control, because you will have faith in yourself, as well as faith in the universe and your place in it. You will know that another can't take whatever you need or desire away. You will believe in your heart of hearts that you are good enough and that you truly do have what you need inside of you to create the life you want to experience.

When you are stuck in controlling everything or everyone around you, just know that you are removing yourself from the very energy that could expand your life beyond what you can envision or dream. Control keeps you tethered to the idea that you are powerless and keeps you from experiencing everything you can be.

Safety Net of Needing to Be Right

*Needing to be right is not
only about safety.
It is also fueled by the need to feel
valued and to prove one's worth.
However, it unfortunately shuts
the door on the Higher Self's ability
to reveal what is most lovingly
appropriate in any given situation.*

The final safety net I will discuss here is the need to be right. You can find this safety net in many people as well as organizations and countries.

> Some believe that if they do their inner work "right," they will avoid any and all bumps in the road. Others believe that because they only eat the "right" foods or do the "right" amount of exercise, they will be kept free from all illness. Still others believe that because they are in the "right" religion, they will be saved from the evils of the world. While they are certainly entitled to

253

believe as they do, they are rarely open to hearing any viewpoint different from their own.

At first glance, these groups may appear very different in their beliefs. I see no difference between any of them. Elitist beliefs in any form are a way to separate ourselves from others. They allow us to feel somehow special and better than other people, to feel safe and above the normal conditions of life, and, most importantly to feel we are right.

Life is fluid. What was right one day may be totally inappropriate another. If we hang on to what we feel is right no matter what, we miss the chance to grow beyond what we have known. Situations change, and therefore we too must be willing to change or risk becoming stuck in old, worn out ways of being. I believe we came here to grow and to expand, so our viewpoints need to grow and expand constantly.[5]

On the way back to self-love, you will have to let go of this need to be right. It can be very hard for people to admit they have this safety net, because they have convinced themselves they *are* right (and therefore everyone else is wrong). It can be very comforting to feel righteous—especially when you feel so wrong inside. However, this "need" masks a feeling of inferiority. It has nothing to do with being better than another and everything to do with feeling as if one is less than another. When you are seated in self-love, you will make choices that feel right for you moment by moment,

---

[5] McClung, J. How Learning to Say Goodbye Taught Me How to Live, 70, 72.

allowing others to do the same with no need to bring them around to your thinking. You will understand that a differing viewpoint is not an attack on your core being. It is just an alternative perspective coming from someone who is looking at the world through different lenses.

As you work with the questions, observe how stubborn you are in relating to the questions and the answers you begin to feel. Your stubbornness will tell you a lot about your addiction to this safety net.

Questions to Investigate

1) How important is it to you to always be right?

_____

_____

_____

_____

2) When is the last time you insisted on being right, and what did it add to your life?

_____

_____

_____

_____

3) How do you handle finding out you are wrong, and what feelings does it bring forward?

_____

_____

_____

_____

4) How quickly do you apologize when you make a mistake or hurt someone?

_____

_____

_____

_____

5) Are you gracious when you are wrong, or do you get mad?

_____

_____

_____

_____

6) Are you comfortable with saying "I am sorry"?

_____

_____

_____

_____

7) Do you enjoy telling someone "I told you so"?

_____

_____

_____

_____

8) Do you try to get everyone around you to believe as you do?

_____

_____

_____

_____

9) How do you respond when someone disagrees with you?

_____

_____

_____

_____

10) Was there anyone in your childhood who mirrored that "need to be right" behavior?

_____

_____

_____

_____

11) How did that behavior make you feel when it was directed at you?

_____

_____

_____

_____

12) Were you shamed or punished when you were wrong about something as a child?

_____

_____

_____

_____

13) As a child, were you allowed to believe differently than your parents or other family members around you?

_____

_____

_____

_____

14) When is the last time you outgrew what you thought was right?

_____

_____

_____

_____

15) What would happen to your world if you allowed others to also be right?

_____

_____

_____

_____

16) Can you consider that perhaps what is right for you is not right for another? If not, why not?

_____

_____

_____

_____

17) How would your life be different if you no longer had to convince people you were right?

_____

_____

_____

_____

18) How would your life be different if you no longer had to convince yourself you are right?

_____

_____

_____

_____

19) When is the last time you admitted, "I don't know"?

_____

_____

_____

_____

20) How capable are you at trusting you will find the appropriate answer or path when you admit you don't know what is right?

_____

_____

_____

_____

21) Can you consider that not knowing the right answer can open you up to new and better experiences? If not, why not?

_____

_____

_____

_____

Final Thought on Needing to Be Right

Our souls are always pushing us to expand beyond what was to what could be, and that means letting go of the idea that what was right once will always be right.

While our egos like to feel superior with their rules and regulations for life, our souls flourish when we remain flexible and open to the ever-changing nature of life. It is that openness to life that will afford our Higher Selves the opportunity to offer us new ideas and solutions for whatever the situation. Where our egos are only able to see black and white, our Higher Selves can see the entire rainbow of colors.[6]

When you move through the world rooted in self-love, you no longer are concerned that people agree with you or that you must win an argument or debate. You understand that everyone must make his or her own decisions on what is right for him or her and how he or she sees his or her world. And when you find someone that is stuck in needing to be right, you will

---

[6] McClung, J. How Learning to Say Goodbye Taught Me How to Live, 72.

not condemn him or her, but instead you will have compassion and empathy for what he or she feels inside, for you too once garnered your value and worth and safety in the same manner.

MEDITATION EXERCISE

Go into your safe space along with your Higher Self and remember a recent time when one of your safety nets got activated. Recall what initial emotion rose up and activated your safety net. Were you feeling threatened, devalued, or invisible? Perhaps you had experienced a recent disappointment or loss.

Then bring forward other times when you engaged in this go-to behavior. What were you feeling then? Were there similar feelings going on inside of you? What was your payoff in that moment? Did it make you feel more valuable or more worthy or powerful?

If you were in judgment, did you gain a sense of comfort from the thought that at least you were better than the other person? If you were in control, did that control temporarily take away your fear that someone might find out you are not good enough or take something away from you? If you fought to be right, did it make you feel superior and more valuable than the other because he or she was wrong and you were right? You will begin to see a pattern to your safety net and what activates it.

Once you have explored what is underneath your safety net, return to the part of you that still doesn't believe he or she is lovable, loving, (good enough), or loved, and work there just as you did before. Dialogue with him or her and bring in your Higher Self to add its wisdom and love to the conversation.

Remind your orphan that whatever happened to him or her that caused him or her to create these safety nets is not indicative of who he or she truly is or how the universe or the divine sees him or her. Allow your orphan to cry and vent; then let him or her know again that he or she is no longer on his or her own. Your orphan now has you, a Higher Self, and a whole universe on his or her side. He or she no longer needs to be afraid. All that pain and fear is over and in the past.

Also let your orphan know you forgive him or her for his or her behavior and that you understand why he or she reacted as he or she did. Your orphan did the best he or she could with what he or she thought was true.

You can also ask for your orphan's forgiveness for your not being aware of him or her before now and having left him or her on his or her own to cope. However, now that you are aware, reiterate that your orphan does not need to be in charge anymore. You, with the help of your Higher Self, will handle life. Your orphan is free.

End your time with this orphan by surrounding him or her with love. You can even send your orphan off to play if he or she likes. This will reinforce the idea that your orphan does not have to worry and be in charge anymore.

Then take some time to feel forgiveness for yourself. Let your Higher Self offer this balm of forgiveness for all you have done while asleep and in pain. Just as you understand why your orphan reacted as he or she did, you now know better what fear and loathing has caused you to do. Receive this forgiveness for yourself and feel the love the universe has and has always had for you breaking though the barriers around your heart.

Okay, put music on if you wish, get comfy and close your eyes, and uncover what is behind your favorite safety nets.

FINAL THOUGHT ON SAFETY NETS

Much like working with an abused or feral animal, it takes patience and time to gain your orphans' trust. They have been on their own for a very long time, so it will not happen in one session. It is a process. However, if you will keep returning to them with kindness, understanding, and compassion, they will come around and trust that you are in charge. They will finally believe that they are safe to relax and breathe again.

While I highlighted only three of the most common safety nets, if your go-to behavior is a "be nice at all cost" demeanor, anger, self-righteousness, or any other protective behavior, the work is the same. You must discover what fear and feelings of self-loathing are running the safety net.

Your safety nets are not about who you are but about how you see the world and what you decided you must do to be safe and feel loved. When your heart is rooted in self-love, safety nets are no longer necessary. The whole point of all of this work is to understand why you feel, believe, and behave the way you do, so you can move out of justifying your pain and move into compassionate understanding.

It is this energy of compassionate understanding that will enable you to take the final step of integrating all your orphaned parts back into the whole, freeing you finally to be who you were always meant to be.

Your Homework

Take notice throughout your week of where and how many times your favorite safety net comes into play. Continue to investigate what triggers this safety net. Also look to see who in your circle also has this safety net. Do you gravitate toward people who also judge others or themselves? If control is your issue, do you mainly associate with people that are easy to control? What about people whom you can't control? Is there a battle of wills that happens when you are with them? Look to how many times you insisted on being right. How far were you willing to go to get that sense of value?

If you find that giving up a certain safety net frightens you, go into meditation and work with the orphan to remind him or her of the truth of who he or she is both to you and to the universe. Keep replacing that false sense of worth, value, and being good enough that the safety nets offer with authentic love and truth.

Work with your Higher Self as well so you can continue to connect the dots regarding what is running this safety net for you. *Feel* compassion being offered to you from your Higher Self for all that you have been through and all that you have done because of it. Continue to find forgiveness for yourself and all your wounded parts.

Take a moment each day to just *feel* love coming into you in all its glorious flavors. Let love wash over you.

During your day, when you witness yourself activating your safety nets, take a deep breath and reject the behavior by declaring, "I don't need to [fill in the blank] any longer." Then silently say the following affirmation:

I know I am safe.
I know I am lovable, loving, and loved beyond measure.
I forgive myself the past, and I choose love.
Love is my power now.

This action will aid you in consciously observing your life and detecting what is going on around you rather than blindly going through your day. It will set your intention on remembering the truth of who you are. It will likewise keep you focused on forgiveness and your ability at any time to choose love over fear.

NOTES

Chapter 12

What is the final step of integration?

The final step of integration is sharing the same forgiveness that you have learned to give yourself through compassionate understanding to all those that have caused you harm.

Integration is the natural byproduct of forgiving the past and replacing fear with the truth of love. You have practiced investigating by paying attention to what is going on inside of you when you are emotionally triggered and by observing your thoughts.

You have practiced interrogating by asking yourself *why* you feel or believe what you do, and by dialoguing with the orphaned parts of yourself to discover what pain or fear they are carrying. All of this work was to get you to a place of integrating these splintered parts back into the whole. And why is that important? As I have said, these orphaned parts not only carry pain but also have pieces of your power, your joy, your creativity, your dreams, your hope and faith and trust, your love of self, the world, and the universe. You cannot fully move into self-love without integrating these orphaned parts back into the whole. Forgiveness is the crucial component to transforming the past and reclaiming your self-love.

By now you understand what your orphans have been feeling and believing about themselves, the world, and the universe, and what has caused you to behave as you do. You have worked with your orphans to have a better understanding of what happened to them and how it was not the truth of how the universe sees them. You have connected with your Higher Self so you can experience what *unconditional* love looks and feels like, helping you to grow in love for all of your selves. Through all of this detective work, you have discovered your ability to practice compassionate understanding with your orphans, as well as with yourself. It is because of this compassionate understanding that you finally were able to begin to find forgiveness within for yourself and all you have done.

By attaining compassionate understanding and moving into forgiveness, you have empowered yourself to choose how you want to see the past as well as how you see yourself, the universe, and your place in it.

Forgiveness acts as the ultimate cleaning agent, removing and dissolving the lies and obstacles that have kept you from the truth that you are a powerful piece of the divine. It affords you the understanding that you always had and will always have—the power to choose to create your experiences from fear and lies or from love and the truth.

Deciding how you choose to see the past is an empowering act. Deciding to forgive the past and all it participants is a liberating act.

Let me be very clear here. Forgiveness does not mean condoning an action or behavior. Nor is it pretending that the action didn't impact you negatively. It is my hope that through all the work you have done thus far, denial will no longer be an option.

Forgiveness is compassionate understanding, and it can't be rushed. You can't force yourself to forgive. It is a process. It will not happen in one meditation. It happens in layers. Just as it took time to get to compassionate understanding for yourself and begin to forgive yourself, it will take time for you to get there for the people in your past. But you will get there.

Okay, I can hear some say, "No way will I ever forgive them. They hurt me too badly. They don't deserve forgiveness!" First off, let me remind you that forgiveness is not about them. It is about you. You may never want to see those people again, and that's fine. But as long as you hold blame, you cannot and will not ever be free. You will be invisibly shackled to them for the rest of your life.

Secondly, if that was your response, it should be clear to you by now that you have more work to do with your orphans. You can't offer forgiveness to another until you have reached compassionate understanding for all of your parts. You can't give another what you refuse to give to yourself. If you have not forgiven yourself, you cannot forgive another.

However, once you have reached forgiveness for yourself, you are going to use the same tools to reach it for others. It is so much easier to forgive a bully in your past when you have owned the fact that you too have been a bully. Just by the fact that you now understand why you behaved as you did, you can begin to understand why others may behave like bullies. It isn't because they are just mean people, but just as you did, they act out of self-loathing. You still may not like their behavior, but you can understand it.

One of the greatest benefits of truthfully knowing yourself inside and out is that it helps you to understand what might be behind other people's actions. When you have acknowledged your lack of self-love and what it has caused you to do, it makes it so much easier to let people off the hook for their lack of self-love and what it has made them do. Let me repeat: you may not want to ever be around them again, but you can let them off the hook which, in turn, lets you off the hook.

I have not found one formula that works across the board. It all depends on what and whom you are working to forgive. Sometimes it is enough to understand that the other person was an alcoholic or mentally or emotionally ill and that their actions had absolutely nothing to do with you. You can find forgiveness for that person because it becomes clear through your homework that he or she was not in his or her "right" mind. While you might not be struggling with an illness, you certainly can own that you have not always been in your "right" mind when you behaved "badly."

Perhaps you are aware of someone's past history of being abused, making it easier for you to understand why that person is the way he or she is now. Through your inner work, you have a deeper understanding of how the fear of being abused, ignored, or disrespected can actually cause someone to put up safety nets that end up creating the behavior of a bully.

Others whose reasons for their actions are unknown may take a bit more work. You may not know why someone bullied you, but you can use your own inner homework to know that, whatever the reason, this person was in pain and self-loathing. Having felt your own pain due to your self-loathing, you can begin to feel compassion for this person.

I know that some will say, "Yes, I had pain, but I never treated anyone as badly as he [or she] treated me." That may well be true. However, by taking ownership of what your level of pain has caused you to do, you can begin to imagine the higher level of pain and sense of powerlessness and worthlessness this person must be carrying to do such horrible things.

Putting yourself in another's shoes is the key. That is one of the reasons it was important to *feel* your way through all of the meditations and homework, as well as practicing to tap into your powerful gift of imagination.

Just as you can't just think your way out of loathing and into self-love, you can't just think your way to forgiveness. You are going to have to use your imagination at times to grasp the pain or negative beliefs this person has been consciously or unconsciously allowing to dictate his or her behavior. If you have done your personal behavior exploration and forgiveness work, you are equipped with everything you need to do the same for others.

If you hit a wall in forgiveness work, you can also call in your Higher Self to aid you. What would this wise and unconditionally loving part of you have to say on the subject?

I know a friend who was almost done with her childhood homework and had forgiven almost all of the negative impact her childhood had had on her. However, she was still having a hard time forgiving her mother for seemingly always choosing peace over protecting her from her sibling. She was confused by her mother's behavior because she knew her mother loved her. She was left wondering why her mother didn't protect her, why her mother chose peace over her daughter, and whether her mother didn't love her as much as she thought. Her actions or lack of actions didn't always match her words of love. It became very confusing for my friend.

So she called in her Higher Self, who in turn had her do an exercise to help her understand the reasons for her mother's lack of protection and seeming choice of peace over her daughter.

The mother, who had passed over, was called into the meditation. My friend used her imagination and saw her mother in front of her. When my friend demanded to know why peace was more important to her than she was, she got an answer that finally set her free.

Her mother quietly said, *I didn't think peace was more important. I thought peace would keep you safe.* With that, my friend was able to forgive her mother.

The point of that story is not to convince you that you can dialogue with people on the other side (although I believe you can) but to illustrate the power of your Higher Self and your imagination to help you find whatever path you need to get to compassion and forgiveness. It didn't matter to my friend if she could prove that the statement was "right" and not just something she was making up to make herself feel better. Hearing those words felt "right," and yes, it did make her feel better!

If you will ask for help to get to forgiveness, your Higher Self will always find a way that works for you. I wrote about one of those ways in my previous a book. I had been having trouble forgiving my best friend, Rob, for something she had done. I could not fathom why she did what she had done. But then I was gifted with a dream that literally had me walk in her shoes.

> Rob was climbing a steep mountain. She had a large sack on her back and was having trouble putting one foot in front of the other as she attempted to climb the mountain. She was tired and barely moving. As I watched the scene, I began to feel what she felt. I could feel the heaviness and weight of the sack on my back and felt that I couldn't carry it much longer. I could barely move my feet. I felt so hopeless, as if I had no choice in the situation. And then the dream was over. When I awoke, any anger and hurt was lifted, and all that remained was compassion for Rob.[7]

Forgiving the past is not about being right. It is about freeing yourself from a detrimental viewpoint of blame, self-loathing, and victimhood and moving to one of compassion, self-love, and empowerment. Using the gifts that you have been given to achieve authentic forgiveness is a sign of a wise person who has discovered the power of self-love and used it for his or her greatest good.

---

[7] McClung, J., How Learning to Say Goodbye Taught Me How to Live, 77

QUESTIONS TO INVESTIGATE

1) Who are the people you need to forgive? Why?

_____

_____

_____

_____

2) What feelings arise when you think about forgiving
   them?

_____

_____

_____

_____

3) Do you believe finding forgiveness means condoning
   bad behavior? If so, why?

_____

_____

_____

_____

4) Do you believe that if you forgive, you might be giving permission for those you need to forgive to treat you in the way you were treated?

_____

_____

_____

_____

5) What has kept you from forgiving them before now?

_____

_____

_____

_____

6) What is your payoff for not forgiving them?

_____

_____

_____

_____

7) What would you have to give up in order to forgive them?

_____

_____

_____

_____

8) Have you ever put yourself in their shoes? If not, why not?

_____

_____

_____

_____

9) Have you ever considered what they think and feel about themselves?

_____

_____

_____

_____

10) Have you ever examined their viewpoint of the world and their place in it?

_____

_____

_____

_____

11) What do they believe about how the universe or divine sees them?

_____

_____

_____

_____

12) Have you ever received forgiveness from another person?

_____

_____

_____

_____

13) How did receiving that forgiveness feel?

_____

_____

_____

_____

14) Have you ever found forgiveness for something someone did to you?

_____

_____

_____

_____

15) How did letting that person off the hook make you feel?

_____

_____

_____

_____

16) Can you believe that by using your gifts of a Higher Self and an imagination you can find understanding and forgiveness? If not, why not?

_____

_____

_____

_____

17) Can you believe that forgiving someone is actually offering yourself freedom? If not, why not?

_____

_____

_____

_____

18) How do you think your life would change if you forgave the people who hurt you?

_____

_____

_____

_____

19) How would your life change if you knew you always had the power to find forgiveness and therefore always had the power to be free to choose how you live and create your life?

_____

_____

_____

_____

Meditation Exercise

Please note that when doing the meditation, if you find that you are venting or spewing emotion toward the person you are working to forgive, you need to stop and go back to the earlier work with the emotions and the orphans. This also holds true if you are waiting for an apology before you are willing to forgive. This just means you have more work to do before you can move into the forgiveness process.

***

Go into your safe space and call in your Higher Self to aid you in moving into compassionate understanding for the person you are working on forgiving. Picture that person in front of you. What is his or her story? If you know his or her story, try *feeling* how this person's life story might have affected him or her.

If you know this person was mistreated or abused as a child, picture him or her as a child. Imagine the fear, pain, and feelings of powerlessness that must have consumed this person. Did life disappointment him or her so much that he or she just gave up?

If you don't know this person's story, remember the times you behaved similarly and the pain and emotions that fueled your behavior. Imagine which emotions are underneath the mask this person shows the world. If this person was full of rage or jealousy, what fears are underneath those emotions? Explore as much as you can with what is going on inside of the person. Use your imagination. You already have discovered what was behind your masks and safety nets, so do the same with him or her. Put yourself in that person's shoes!

If the person has passed over, call him or her into your meditation and dialogue with him or her. If the person is still here, you can call in his or her Higher Self to help you get understanding on the situation. Trust your imagination. It will aid you greatly in the process.

You want to get to the understanding that while the person may have been damaged or flawed, he or she was just doing the best he or she could with all the pain and fear he or she was stuffing deep inside. Just like you, this person lost the truth of who he or she was and replaced it with lies. So be willing to feel this person's pain.

End your meditation by sending this person love, letting him or her know you better understand what life felt like for him or her. And if you are ready, let the person know you are sorry for his or her pain. Then take some time to feel love coming into your heart.

When you eventually get to forgiveness for this person, envision love enveloping both of you, removing any ties tangled around each of you that are keeping you connected to one another. Picture your energy separating from this person.

Then see a light of love surround and fill your heart. Feel the sense of freedom this forgiveness brings. *Feel* the power that is your loving heart. Celebrate this power, this heart, and celebrate that you have chosen love over fear and empowerment over victimhood.

Finally, thank yourself, your Higher Self, and the universe for the healing energy of forgiveness.

Okay, put music on if you wish, get comfy, and close your eyes and begin to free yourself by forgiving the past.

Final Thought

Remember: forgiveness can't be rushed. It tends to be done in layers. You will know when you have authentically forgiven the person because you will feel it break open your heart, and the tears will flow. You will feel like a ten-ton weight has been lifted. You will also notice that you are no longer afraid of this person or no longer feel any anger toward him or her. You may not want to see the person, but it will not be because you are afraid him or her or fear what emotions may be triggered when in this person's presence. When you practice forgiveness, you are actively taking your power back, enabling you to make choices out of love and not fear.

After forgiving someone, don't be surprised if you have to turn around and forgive yourself for not having done it sooner. That's okay. Just make sure you do it. You don't want to miss out on receiving the liberating energy of forgiveness for yourself.

When we practice compassionate understanding, forgiving ourselves, and forgiving others for all mistakes and trespasses, we open up a space for love to blossom. It is through this blossoming love that we will discover our true power to choose love in all we see and do. We will know without a doubt that we are lovable, loving, and loved, as is every single person on this beautiful planet, because we have discovered the truth within.

Your Homework

Throughout your week, notice when revenge or blame is admired or even celebrated over forgiveness. Pay attention to how that kind of thinking has affected the people who are relishing the idea of revenge.

Go into meditation and continue to gather understanding for the person you want to forgive. Constantly put yourself in that person's shoes. If you keep focusing on finding forgiveness, trust that your Higher Self and the universe will aid in whatever way you need to get there.

You can look for people in your daily life who may have energy similar to that of the person you are working to forgive. The universe has a wonderful way of putting the right people in our faces to teach and help us on our journeys. Since these people are not the ones who caused you pain, it will be easier to find compassionate understanding for them. You then can use that information to help you understand the person you are working to forgive.

Also continue to open yourself up to receiving more love and forgiveness for yourself. You have a tremendous reservoir of love right inside of you. You just have to tap into to feel its life-affirming impact.

During the day, keep your intention on the energy of forgiveness and silently affirm the following:

I am no longer a victim.
I am choosing to forgive the past and all participants.
I know I have everything inside of
me to achieve this freedom.
And I know I have my Higher Self helping in this goal.

This action will set your intention on forgiving and remind you that you are more than capable of achieving this freedom.

NOTES

Chapter 13

What's next once I have integrated my orphans and forgiven the past?

The next step is practicing your self-love out in the "real" world. You also are going to continue to expand your beliefs as you continue to develop your understanding of love and its power.

While the healing of our inner orphans and the core beliefs they have been carrying reaches completion once we have arrived at compassionate understanding and forgiveness, the practice of self-love is a lifetime endeavor. You will always find new ways to expand and grow your sense of self-love and the expression of that love out in the world.

You will continue to use the tools you have acquired to change beliefs that are too constricting, to develop deeper levels of self-awareness and compassion, and to increase your ability to feel love from within, as well as your ability to receive love. The discovery and the connection to your inner world, to your Higher Self, and to the orphan parts of yourself was just the beginning. While the beginning steps are the most difficult and painful, they are also the most important steps.

You needed to realize that the power to heal and to make changes within begins and ends with you. You needed to come to the realization that you are the only one who gets to decide what you believe and how you choose to see yourself, the world, and the universe or the divine. You needed to rediscover and learn to use the tools you were gifted with, such as imagination, emotions, and your Higher Self. You needed to identify and tap into the infinite wellspring of love that has always resided within you and begin to build a trust that it will always be available to drink from at any time. All of this was to give you a new sense of empowerment and faith in your ability to find what you need within.

The redefining of self-love and orphan work was to heal your core wounds, change your core negative beliefs to more loving beliefs, and to help you authentically let go of the past through forgiveness. It was to allow these orphaned parts, through your love, to finally let go and let you be in charge of your life.

While the orphan work does come to an end once the past is forgiven and your orphans know they are safe and loved and that you are in charge now, you should be aware you most likely will experience what I call "pop tests" for a short period afterward. What I mean by pop tests is that you might find yourself in certain circumstances that trigger an old familiar feeling from your past. It won't be anywhere as strong as it used to be, but it will be there nonetheless. Please note that if the feeling is just as strong as before, it means you have more healing and orphan work to do.

Pop tests are chances to practice out in the world what you have been practicing within. It would be great if once we were done we never had to be around the old energies again, but it doesn't seem to work that way. The universe, in its infinite wisdom, knows we need to practice our new level of self-awareness and love out in the "real" world. It is a way for us not only to build trust in ourselves but also to experience our growth firsthand, which in turn will empower us to grow even further.

When I had completed my orphan work and taken back my power from being afraid of angry people (one of my core issues), what did the universe do? It brought me face-to-face with people who were angry. While I didn't feel anywhere close to the fear I used to feel, I did have a small internal reaction. Luckily, I knew that these pop tests were simply ways for me to witness how I now handle these old energies that I had felt so powerless against in the past.

The first thing I noticed was that I did not immediately respond to the anger, which I would have done in the past to protect myself either by being apologetic—even if I didn't do anything—just to make it end or by puffing up and pushing against the anger being directed at me.

The second thing I noticed was that I did not take responsibility for the other person's anger. I knew that person's anger wasn't my fault, which was a huge change for me and was vital in healing my orphan. The pop tests confirmed for me that I had indeed healed that wound and the beliefs that came out of it.

The third thing I noticed was that while my stomach may have initially clenched (an old knee-jerk reaction), I was able to relax it almost immediately. No longer was I unsure of my safety or lovability or value. These new feelings of self-love afforded my body the assurance that it was safe and didn't need to clench. With one deep breath, my body would relax.

And lastly, and most importantly, I noticed that with each new pop test, I grew in my self-trust that I could stay centered in my self-love and make choices based on that love and not on fear or other people's energies.

You are going to have pop tests every time you make a major change within, but try to remember it is a good thing. It just means you have done the heavy lifting within and now get to witness those changes firsthand. The trust you have in yourself and the trust you have in your inner work will grow with each pop test until you no longer need a pop test to know you have changed and grown in love in that particular area. Just as suddenly as the pop tests appear, they will disappear.

You're also going to discover that there is always room for you to grow in self-love. Once you have redefined love for yourself and have completed the integration of your orphans, you are going to feel liberated—and you should. It is a powerful thing to be free from that past. It is going to feel as if you were lifted out of a dark hole and placed on a higher plateau where the air is sweet.

However, eventually that plateau is going to begin to feel flat; and the air, less sweet. I can hear many of you shouting, "Why is that? Shouldn't that feeling last? After all, I worked so hard to get there." I would have to respond, "No, and you don't really want it to!" While you may be free from the past and the dark hole forever— and for some that will be enough—you are going to come up against a growth edge if you have a desire to continue to grow and expand your definition of love and ability to feel love. However, don't let that frighten you. Growth edges are not in any way as intense as the orphan work.

You encounter a growth edge when you butt up against beliefs or viewpoints that were okay or workable for a while but now no longer suit you. Think of your beliefs as being like a box or container. Your beliefs create a box around you, allowing you to move freely within that box. The good news is that you have just expanded this box with much of the work you did in redefining self-love and changing your core beliefs.

With that belief work and the healing and integration of your orphans, you rose to a new plateau. I call it rising to a new plateau of love and understanding, and it feels great. You actually feel so free and more your true self. Then months go by, and you begin to have new dreams and new desires that you want to explore, and suddenly that box of beliefs doesn't feel so freeing. It begins to feel too tight and constricting. Why is that? Your current box of beliefs is unable to support your new vision.

Now the plateau of love that once felt so high and expansive feels flat and full of stale air. This isn't because you didn't do good work before, so don't despair. It simply means that you are ready to rise to a new plateau of love and understanding, and in order to do so, you must expand your box of beliefs to get there.

See if this helps. Let's say you changed a belief in your orphan work from "The universe doesn't care about me" to "The universe does care about me." It certainly is much better to believe that the universe cares about you than to believe it doesn't. This new belief expanded your box, and it felt great and was possibly enough to help you integrate one of your orphans.

However, now with new dreams and desires born out of your increasing self-love, you discover that the universe caring about you is not enough to help you believe you can have the dreams you want. So now you must expand the idea that the universe cares about you to "The universe also cares about my dreams."

This expands your box and feelings of love until that belief becomes too small. Then you change that belief to include not only "cares about my dreams" but also "wants me to have dreams"—a bigger box and more love. Then, farther down the road, you may decide that's not big enough and add "The universe is actively aiding me in achieving my dreams"—an even bigger box and even more love.

As you can see, each step expands your box, eventually raising you to a new plateau of love and understanding until it is time to expand and rise again.

You will have to practice patience with yourself on your belief work. Because beliefs or new viewpoints must be rooted in the heart, very few of us are able to jump from believing the universe doesn't care about us to believing the universe loves us and values our dreams so much that it is doing everything to aid us in creating all our dreams or something even better. The jump is too big for most of us.

Many of us have spent years within a certain box, cultivating the beliefs forming that box. To go from an extra-small box to a supersized box would feel uncomfortable and even frightening. We may mentally be able to buy it and want it, but the heart will need time and loving care, just as your orphans did, to catch up. But it will catch up!

Rather than getting upset when you hit a growth edge, try to see it as a nudge from your Higher Self indicating that it is time and you are ready now to expand and widen your beliefs so you can experience even more love in your life.

By now you should know you don't have to do this alone. You have everything you need to grow right inside of you, along with the tools to do it. You will work with your Higher Self to continually expand your definitions of love, the universe, and your own power within the universe, just as you did when working with your orphans. You will continue opening your heart and expanding your capability to feel more and more love in all its glorious flavors.

While self-love is a state of being, the expression of that love through your dreams and desires will constantly be changing and increasing. You will always have the opportunity to rise to new and higher plateaus of love and deeper understandings on the power of love.

There is no limit to the amount of love your heart can experience. The only limit is the one you put on it. While the goal may no longer be to remove the walls around the heart that were formed out of your wounds, there will always be ways to expand and empower the heart to new levels of feeling and expressing the love that is you.

As I have said many times, you come into this world with everything you will ever need for your journey toward love. One of the most beautiful benefits of reclaiming your self-love is that it opens you up to other powerful and loving parts of yourself that were drowned out by your orphans' pain. Unlike the orphan work, which dealt with healing your pain, reconnecting with these loving parts, which certainly can present their own challenges, will nonetheless be exciting and fun.

These delightful and very powerful parts of yourself have just been waiting for you to reclaim your self-love so they can reveal themselves to you and begin to help you express and create through love. While the discussion of these parts could fill a whole book, I figured you deserved to know that there is good stuff still ahead in your inner work.

As you move through the world with the knowledge that you are lovable, loving, and loved, don't be surprised if you're asked where you found this new sense of self-love and empowerment? You can confidently reply, "The same place you will. I journeyed within and discovered that the love I had been desperately seeking was inside me all along."

Chapter 14

*C*an I get a description of one of the
loving parts waiting to be discovered,
and perhaps a hint of what is to come?

Your Magical Child is the part of you that is pure, unfiltered joy and knows the power of that joy.

If you are like me, it is easier for you to do the hard work when you are given a little tease of what is ahead if you continue with your inner explorations. Needless to say, my hope is that you will continue, which is why I want to give you a small taste of one of these powerful and loving parts, the Magical Child.

The Magical Child is not a new concept. Both psychologists and students of archetypes and mythology have discussed its attributes for decades. It is often referred to as "the enchanted one" or "the innocent one."

I am going to discuss just a little of it here in a personal and spiritual manner. Just as your orphans have impacted your life in a variety of negative ways, your Magical Child can impact your life in a variety of positive ways. Think of it this way: if your Higher Self is the one who teaches you about love and the power of love, it is your Magical Child that will teach you about joy and the power of joy.

So who is this Magical Child? Your Magical Child is the best representation of who you are on a soul level. The Magical Child is the part of your soul that comes in with you into this life and holds your joy, excitement, and unwavering faith in love and goodness. It is the closest thing to experiencing your soul while still in human form.

While you may experience wounding during life, creating orphaned parts of yourself, your Magical Child remains pristine. Now, that is not to say it can't get lost for a bit through neglect or get covered up by your orphans or wounds, but it is never damaged. It is your insurance policy, so to speak, against your ego and whatever life may throw at you. Because it is the best representation of who you truly are on a soul level, it is the best way for you to stay connected to the truth of who you are and to use that truth to create your experiences. Believe it or not, underneath all your scrapes and bruises, you are a joyous being!

While we may call this energy or aspect of our souls the Magical Child, it is not a child in its wisdom and power. Perhaps the reason we identify this energy with a child is that very few of us are able to experience joy or have unshakable faith as freely as an innocent child does. An innocent child trusts in the universe and lives moment by moment with no worry as to what the next moment might bring. An innocent child believes in the innate goodness of life. He or she has the ability to see beauty where others only see ugliness. He or she can always find the light where others see only darkness. An innocent child believes in unlimited possibilities and can see the magic that is in everything.

Your Magical Child is the part of you that knows it belongs in this world and that this world also belongs to it. Your Magical Child is full of wonder and curiosity. It is always open to new experiences and never fears the unknown but instead is excited by it. It is thrilled to be alive and experience all the flavors of joy this life can afford.

Your Magical Child never doubts itself, because it has always been rooted in the truth that it is lovable, loving, and loved, which is the source of its limitless joy. It has a lust for life and sees life as a boundless adventure.

Your Magical Child's power lies in its connection to divine joy, which remains unfiltered by life. Okay, some may be thinking, "How is joy a power?" Well, if you discovered anything in your orphan work, it is that emotions have power. They are so powerful that they created whole belief systems that have dictated what you create and what you experience. Having said that, can you even imagine what you could create and experience if you were using the power of joy to dictate the outcome of a dream you wish to manifest?

There is much more that can be said about the Magical Child, but as I said, that could be a whole book on its own. I just wanted to give a small hint of the good things that are still waiting to be discovered within your inner world. I will add one more tease, however: if your orphans created your past experiences, it will be your Magical Child that you will team up with to create your future experiences.

The Heart of the Matter is
that you are lovable, loving,
and loved. You always have
been, and you always will
be, and there is nothing
you can do or say that will
ever change that truth.
Isn't it time you believed it?

Made in the USA
Coppell, TX
28 June 2020

29493680R00198